For Joe Flagg with love

COOKING SZECHUAN-STYLE

COOKING SZECHUAN-STYLE

Louise Stallard

DRAKE PUBLISHERS INC.
NEW YORK

Published in 1973 by
Drake Publishers Inc.
381 Park Avenue South
New York, N.Y. 10016

Library of Congress Catalog Card Number 72-10490
ISBN 0-87749-422-3

Printed in Italy

Prepared and produced for the publisher by BMG Productions,
Incorporated

Photographs by Meryl Joseph

CONTENTS

ACKNOWLEDGEMENTS

The author wishes to express her thanks and gratitude to Pao Peter Lee for all his help in the preparation of this book, both text and photographs, and to the Flower Drum Restaurant and its staff. Deep appreciation also to Harry Shum, former manager, and to the staff of the Hunam Restaurant and to Rhona Bross whose kitchens appear in many photographs in this book. Special thanks as well to Joyce Garrick for her help and patience.

COOKING SZECHUAN-STYLE

BEFORE YOU BEGIN

Most of us in the Western world think of "Chinese" food as Cantonese (Canton, nearest to Hong Kong) or Mandarin (Peking, with its advantages as an imperial capital), but over many centuries, most of them before Western civilization was more than a hope, the part of China we know as the provinces of Szechuan, Hunan, and Kweichow developed an entirely different cuisine. Delicious and nutritious, it used the materials available and skirted the limitations; it was, in the mathematical sense, the "elegant solution."

One of this cuisine's major truimphs was its managing to get along without salt. Far inland, the "western provinces" (they *were* west of the old capitals of China) were cut off from coastal products, while their own salt deposits were difficult to mine. Very little salt made its way over the long trails, and none of that reached common people. If there could be no salt for savor, there had to be a substitute: pepper! Many varieties of pepper, both fresh and dried, sweet spices, and soy sauce were used to make saltless food palatable, and a body of wonderful new tastes evolved.

Though Szechuan cooking is new to the Western world, it has long been a favorite of gourmets all over China. An elderly friend who was a student many, many years ago described his rambles through Shanghai and Peking: "We would see the signs on restaurants from the provinces, and we would say, 'So?' but when we found Szechuan cooking, we said, 'Ahhhhh.' "

If you are not familiar with Szechuan food, you will be struck by its differences from Cantonese. First, far from being rather bland, much Szechuan food is spicy, and many dishes are very hot with chilis. Second, much more meat is used; main dishes have just about the opposite proportions of meat to vegetables from that found in Cantonese food. After a Szechuan dinner, you will certainly not feel hungry any time soon! Less cornstarch is used for thickening; sauces are more often cooked down and served slightly thinner than in Cantonese dishes. If you have disliked the texture of thickened sauces, Szechuan cooking will be a pleasant change. Rice is the staple starch, but Szechuan cuisine does not feature noodle dishes as does Cantonese.

Many Cantonese dishes use seafood since it is plentiful there. If so varied a cuisine can be said to have a basic ingredient, Szechuan cooking may be said to be based on poultry. Pork is also popular, but beef is not used very much, nor is it anywhere in China. Bovine animals carry burdens and help cultivate the land; they are (and always were) too valuable to eat. Seafood was not available until recent days of fast transportation and refrigeration, but freshwater fish abounds in the lakes and streams of Szechuan. Freshwater shrimp is a treat most of us can only dream of, but it exists in Szechuan! Many of the vegetables available in the West (and some that are not) are used in Szechuan cooking; vegetables are usually combined with meats, but gently cooked by any of several methods, they can take major roles on the menu. More important than the specific vegetable chosen is its condition; long before science proved it, the Chinese knew that dry, shriveled vegetables were a loss nutritionally and esthetically.

Lively spices, especially chilis of many kinds, distinguish Szechuan cooking. It is always something of a problem to decide what to call the peppers. This book has opted for the Latin American names since they are more widely (and uniformly) used than Chinese names in the West. Fresh hot peppers are sometimes available in vegetable stores or stores serving the Latin American community. These are the ones you are most likely to see.

Chilis serranos are small (1″ to 3″), very dark green shiny peppers with pointed tips; very, very hot.

Chilis Jalapeños are rather like serranos but with blunter ends and usually a little larger; both serranos and Jalapeños are available canned. Be sure to buy the chilis preserved only in water and salt; the pickled ones make the dishes taste very different.

Hot green Italian peppers are long, skinny, and bright green; these peppers are very hot.

Chilis poblanos are much like bell peppers, though usually darker green and longer. Poblanos can be hot, however; always taste before committing yourself.

Red and green bell peppers—the old familiar ones.

Several varieties of dried hot peppers are also used.

Szechuan pepper, also known as *fagara*, comes as rough reddish-brown peppercorns slightly smaller than black peppercorns. It has a mild peppery, spicy taste somewhat like cinnamon with a bite. In Chinese or Japanese food stores it may be labeled simply "Peppercorns"; sniff and bite into one of them to make sure.

Chilis pasillas are long (4″ to 8″) thin black peppers. They are very tasty but very hot. They come dry and very hard, but they will soften in a few minutes in very hot water.

Chilis pequines are very small (about the size of apple seeds) orange-red *very* hot peppers. The amount called for will sound small, but be careful about adding more. They are really fiery!

Chilis Japonesas look like light-red small (1″ or so) hot Italian peppers. Their flavor is interesting, and usually they are not as hot as pequin or pasilla peppers.

Ground cayenne pepper (red pepper) is called for in some recipes, and it may also be used as a substitute when other hot peppers aren't available.

Fresh hot peppers are very perishable; they will go soft and rot in a few days in the refrigerator and much sooner at room temperature. Buy them in small batches. If you need to stock up, wash the peppers quickly, then dip quickly into boiling water, drain, and dry well. Pack into small plastic freezing bags and seal tightly. Freeze at once and keep frozen hard until needed.

Dry and canned peppers will keep almost indefinitely. Keep dry chilis in a dry place to prevent mold.

Fresh ginger is an important ingredient in many Szechuan dishes. It is seasonal and perishable (it dries up at room temperature, molds and eventually rots in the refrigerator; the mold is harmless—just cut it off) but is often available at Chinese grocery stores and sometimes at good vegetable or specialty shops. Perhaps if you ask, a store near you will stock it. A very canny cook suggested that you ask the local Chinese restaurant about its source of supply.

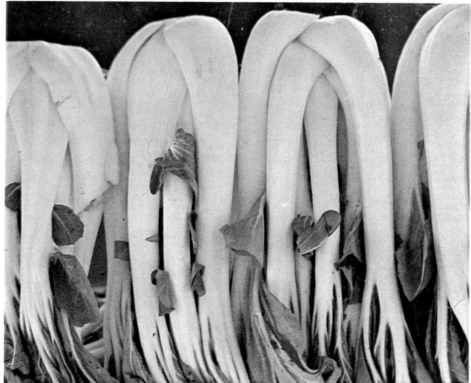

Chinese cabbage (above); Bok choy (below)

You might even be able to buy some from the restaurant. If you cannot find ginger locally, you may send for it by mail. (See Sources.)

Ginger roots look like complex new potatoes; the pieces may be slim as a pencil or almost as large as a potato. It is the total amount of the spice that counts, not its shape, of course, though larger pieces are easier to clean. Some authorities say to peel the ginger, but that is almost impossible. Rub as much of the dry papery skin away as you can—on large pieces a plastic scrubber is helpful—then rinse and use. If you need to store fresh ginger for more than a day or two, wrap it in foil *before washing* and keep in the refrigerator. If the ginger is to be kept more than a week, seal it tightly in foil and freeze whole. Cut the amount needed from the frozen ginger root as you use it.

In most recipes that call for fresh ginger, dried ginger will not give good results. When a substitute is possible, it is noted in the recipe. Dry ginger is a useful spice, however, and you will want to have it on hand. The whole pieces that you grate as you need it taste better than ground ginger, though the ground spice is certainly handy. Buy it in small boxes and plan to use it promptly.

Fresh coriander, also called Chinese parsley, looks rather like broad-leaf parsley but has a different taste entirely. If you have not tried coriander, taste it. Some people love it, but some do not like it at all. It is not hot but gives a subtle and (my vote) intriguing taste. It is sold at Chinese groceries or vegetable or specialty stores in bunches about the size of a bunch of celery but with an important difference: The coriander sprigs will have the roots still attached. Coriander can be kept in the refrigerator for a few days if it is placed in a paper (not plastic) bag *unwashed* and with the *roots on*. It will rot with amazing speed if it is washed before storing. To keep coriander longer, pick the best leaves and stems from the bunch (remove the roots and discard), then quickly wash and dry with paper towels. Freeze at once and store in tightly sealed small plastic bags.

Soy sauce is a basic ingredient in Szechuan cooking. The recipes in this book were developed using Kikkoman-brand Japanese soy sauce, which is thinner, less sweet, and saltier than Chinese soy sauce. The choice is really a matter for each cook to decide. A quick taste for seasonings, a good idea, anyway, will tell whether any adjustments need to be made.

Dried mushrooms are now available in many supermarkets, though the chances are that they will be from Italy instead of China. Not to worry; they work fine. If you do have access to a Chinese grocery, however, you will enjoy shopping and sampling the many different varieties of dried mushrooms available there. Fresh mushrooms are not usually interchangeable with dry ones in the recipes in this book. Such a substitution might work technically, but a very different dish would result.

Dried shrimp, dried lily flowers, and *rice wine* are usually available only at Oriental food stores, but the shrimp and the lily flowers are light to mail, very stable, and should keep almost forever. Sake, usually more widely available than Chinese rice wine, is an acceptable substitute, but the taste of dishes made with it will be a little different.

Saltpeter is needed for smoked duck and large-scale pork curing. It is available at the drug store. Do not send your teen-ager to buy it, however; saltpeter can be an ingredient in bombs, and you wouldn't want to have to get the kid out of police custody!

So you see, not so many unusual or hard-to-get ingredients are necessary to cook Szechuan style. One hot pepper can be substituted for another; coriander is politely declined by some people, anyway. The only ingredient likely to be a real problem is fresh ginger, and since it can be frozen, you need find it only now and then. Then you will have everything on hand to explore Szechuan food.

EQUIPMENT

You do not need exotic equipment to cook Szechuan style. Most of the equipment you will use you have already, tried and true. The real basics are those essential to good cooking anywhere.

Most important of all, you should have a dependable, controllable heat source. A gas flame is my choice, but the fastest electric element may work for you. Some dishes, such as very delicate vegetables and chicken velvet, for instance, require very closely regulated heat; an alcohol or butane flame would be a good investment if you usually cook with electricity.

So much of the cooking in these recipes requires split-second timing that a good minute minder and a clock with a sweep second hand are invaluable.

Since a dizzying number of ingredients in Szechuan recipes need to be finely sliced, shredded, or minced, cooking would be burdensome indeed without good knives and a good cutting board. Your knives should be the best quality you can afford, and then you should take care of them as you do your jewels. Never use them on hard surfaces and never let them soak. Have them sharpened by someone who knows what he is about as often as necessary. If you ask nicely, perhaps the knife-sharpening expert will show you how you can keep the edges up to snuff with a hand stone between his overhauls. It is quality, not quantity, you want in knives; one large knife and one small one are basic—and may be all you need.

Chinese chefs and experienced cooks use 1-pound cleavers for much of the cutting and chopping done to prepare these dishes. It is certainly true that a cleaver (or two used in tandem, a truly alarming sight) in the hands of an experienced cook is a very efficient tool. It is equally true, unfortunately, that it can do a lot of damage while said cook is getting experienced. If you essay a cleaver, take care and go slowly. Remember to use it in moderation; if you hack up the surface of the cutting board severely, splinters will begin to work out and mingle with the food you are chopping. Remember, too, that if you hack heavy bones, chips are going to fly. Wear safety glasses. If this advice sounds alarmist, you clearly have never had a beef-bone chip removed from your cornea.

A compromise method of cutting that allows processes usually reserved to the cleaver, such as hacking a whole chicken or duck, is heavy-knife-and-mallet. This belt-plus-suspenders process allows the person doing the cutting to place the cutting edge of the knife exactly where it should go, then whack it smartly on the back with the mallet, thereby cutting neatly through almost anything the cleaver will cut. You would not use one of your best knives here (nor your best mallet), but a sturdy butcher knife will do fine. And it is quite difficult to hurt yourself.

Chinese cooks and restaurants use *woks* as one of their basic cooking vessels. Shaped like an upside-down coolie hat, a wok distributes heat and provides several different cooking surfaces in one

Assorted vegetables

utensil. The wok is placed on a ring or stand over the heat source, then oil is added. Foods can be cooked quickly in the oil or moved up the shallow side of the wok to drain or cook more slowly. The wok is truly a wonderful pan. If you decide to get one, look for heavy construction and a fairly shallow shape. Get a wok bigger than you think you need; the tiny (7″ or so) woks are cute, but they provide a tiny cooking surface. Look for at least a 12″ wok; a bigger one is even better. It should have a lid. Be sure to get the ring stand, too.

It is possible to use a conventional large skillet instead of a wok, however, and its advantage is that you probably have it already, well seasoned and familiar. By all means get a wok if you want to, but in the meantime a skillet will work fine.

You will need a really large heavy pot for some of the recipes. If it has a rack and a good heavy lid, it can become a steamer as well. A smaller pot goes on the rack, which holds it out of the water in the larger pot, and the lid goes on. Presto! A steamer.

In addition to the usual kitchen equipment, such as a double boiler, some slotted spoons, a sieve, and a cooking fork with a long handle, it is useful to have a really long wooden stirring spoon (to get to the bottom of that *big* pot) and some cheesecloth, which is always handy here and there. If you can use chopsticks, keep several sets to use in cooking. They are really the best implements for the preparation of many dishes in this book. A blender is very nice to have; in fact, it is an almost-essential. A food mill or small meat grinder would be a convenience but is less often used than the blender. A garlic press is a convenience, and a long European-style rolling pin can make all the difference in getting pancakes rolled thin.

Serving platters and bowls are not exactly cooking equipment, but an attractive selection of these dishes can make quite a lot of difference in the way your delicious Szechuan meal *appears*. If you don't have them already, this would be a good time to look for some dark, some light-colored, some ornate, and some plain serving dishes. One of my favorites, for instance, is a dark blue oval dish. Chicken, shrimp, pork, or any light-colored meat dish looks twice as good on it as it would on a white platter.

A cooking-serving pot you will find most useful is one that can be used on the stove, then be carried to the table or buffet to serve an important soup. Many kinds are available; suit your own taste.

My experience has been that large earthenware pots are light and easy to cook in since they distribute heat evenly and slowly (it is hard to make one boil over) and can be very handsome. On the other hand, a very good cook I know dotes on her porcelain-coated iron pot; it is a beauty, too, but it does require a strong man to move it once it is full of soup. Consider your resources of all kinds, then choose.

Porcelain soup spoons are a thoughtful and attractive addition to your table; they are available in Oriental stores and may be very simple and inexpensive or very ornate and quite expensive. In addition to looking pretty, they are very good to eat hot soup with since the porcelain does not conduct heat from the bowl to the handle as metal spoons do. Also, the broad, shallow bowl helps cool each bite of soup as you are about to eat it. You will probably find that you use your porcelain soup spoons for other (purely Western) purposes as well: They make perfect sauce and jelly spoons.

Chopsticks are ideal for eating Szechuan food. If you provide them, you may be surprised how many of your guests are able and willing to use them. If you do get chopsticks, avoid the silver and ivory ones or anything fancy. True elegance in chopsticks is a brand-new set of wooden ones for each guest. Since chopsticks are so inexpensive, you can easily make this gesture. (Of course, chopsticks can be washed and used again; keep the slightly used ones for cooking.) Needless to say, if anyone at your table is uncomfortable with chopsticks, provide forks at once. It is very trying to have to learn a new skill in public (and without any warning). You want your meal to be an occasion for enjoyment of good company and delicious food, not a manual dexterity test.

COOKING METHODS

Most of the recipes in this book have one factor in their cooking methods in common: They are *fast*. Please, please always read the recipe through before planning to cook it or beginning its preparation. That way you can avoid the plight of a friend of mine who had three couples in her living room at the end of their third drinks when she went to bring her very ambitious dinner (from the big red leather *Gourmet Cook Book*) to a finish. Imagine her distress when the next paragraph said, "Store in a cool dark place for 36 hours."

Many main-dish recipes are cooked by stir frying, cooking thinly sliced (or chopped) ingredients in very hot oil in a wok or skillet for a very short time. This is not a difficult technique if you follow some simple precautions. First, you must have a dependable and controllable heat source. Then, *all ingredients must be prepared and ready before you begin to cook*. It is impossible to stress this requirement too strongly. The cooking process goes so fast that once it has begun, there is no time to cut or prepare ingredients to be added later.

Since the ingredients must be prepared ahead, anyway, stir frying lends itself to cooking at the table or buffet. The cut vegetables and meats will look very attractive arrayed on small plates around your chafing dish, and you will look glamorous and efficient whipping up a dish before the guests' eyes.

And since several ingredients usually need preparation, these recipes are good ones to enlist your family in helping to prepare. But play fair! A certain mother who will remain nameless used to hand me a very ripe tomato and a very dull knife. "Nice thin slices, dear," she would say. Well, it couldn't be done. But even the smallest child (who is interested) can safely take the chicken meat off the bones or break beans.

Light vegetable oil, such as peanut oil (the choice of many of the best Chinese cooks), safflower oil, or top-quality lard, is usually used for stir frying. Some dishes taste better with one or the other, and those recipes so state. Very good lard is packed by the major meat-packing houses and should be available at your supermarket or butcher. If you have a local slaughterhouse that handles pigs, they may have fresh lard; if so, do try it. Ask for leaf lard, the most delicate kind—it makes very good piecrust and biscuits as well. Whatever shortening you choose, it should be fresh, of course. It should be very hot, but not burning, when other ingredients are added. If it burns, wash the pan and start over. The taste of burned oil is pretty awful. Be miserly with the oil at the beginning of the cooking process. You can add a bit more later if necessary. Except for a few vegetable dishes, you should not have any oil to pour

Assorted peppers

off at the end of the cooking process. Keep in mind that all the oil you put in the pan is going to be *eaten* and stay your hand.

Just as you need to have all the ingredients ready before you begin to cook, it is also a good idea to have your diners on hand. Most of the dishes in this book will not wait or at least won't wait very long. If you have to serve a dinner at an uncertain time, consider one of the hearty soups or do the cooking itself after the crowd is actually in view. A few dishes really can't be held, and their recipes so note.

MEALS AND MENUS

The traditional Chinese pattern of eating includes an early breakfast (very unlike ours) and two other meals of equal size and importance; there is no "lunch" as distinct from "dinner." One of these important meals for eight people would usually consist of six or eight main dishes plus a soup eaten throughout the meal and rice (but usually not a desert). It is to be hoped that the main dishes would represent a nice balance of meat dishes, fish dishes, and vegetable dishes. More elaborate meals for special occasions or formal entertaining can go to all lengths.

A meal for people used to eating non-Chinese style should probably be considerably less elaborate. A good rule of thumb is one stir-fry dish for each 1½ diners, with any awkward arithmetic resolved in the direction of your guests' appetites. Four hearty eaters would get three dishes; four ladies watching their weights would get two. The stir-fry recipes in this book (those calling for about ½ pound of meat) make one dish of the kind we are discussing. If you want more of one dish, cook two batches instead of doubling the recipe. A crowded skillet won't cook properly.

If you do not have them already, you will want to get some smaller and some larger soup bowls. These bowls (the smaller ones for clear soups and those served between the courses as taste breaks; the larger ones for important main-dish soups) should be fairly deep as opposed to, say, cream soup plates. In China there would not be plates under the bowls, but you may want to use them. They surely save on linen laundry!

Soup is not usually a first course in China but instead is eaten throughout the meal and between courses. If you do serve soup first, carefully balance it with the rest of the meal so that it doesn't kill the appetite for and the taste of the foods to follow. For instance, a peppery-hot shin of beef soup would completely defeat delicate chicken velvet; a hearty thickened soup would kill appetites effectively. If you serve it throughout the meal, the soup should be a contrast to the other dishes: light and delicate to break a series of spicy dishes, spicy to enliven bland ones.

In planning a menu overall, there are two important factors to consider. The first is who you are feeding. What are their tastes? Will they take kindly to new dishes? Do they like hot spicy foods? Are they on restrictive diets? Have they religious dietary restrictions? The best meal in the world will not be successful if these questions are not considered. You can certainly serve some adventurous dishes, but make sure there is something everyone can enjoy. One hot dish among a selection of more familiar offerings may even make some converts! And devotees of spicy food can concentrate on it. You will want to exercise your own judgment about amounts of chilis and spices. Don't be intimidated by the recipes; you know your group best.

The second consideration is *contrast*. A meal made up entirely of hot spicy dishes would be like an aria of unrelieved high Cs: nobody could stand it. In fact, three hot dishes are probably the practical limit even in elaborate meals, and even those three should not be alike in main ingredients, spice, and texture. More than three hot dishes get to tasting alike, just as too many perfumes sampled at once lose their scent. With the recipes available, it is not difficult to choose dishes that contrast in color, dominant flavor, texture, and even temperature. Consider also the colors in each dish; an interesting combination will make the food *seem* to taste better. If your meal is to be served in courses, make sure there is contrast between them, too.

The presentation of food is important to its enjoyment, a factor too often overlooked in Western dining. Give careful consideration to the way your Chinese dishes are served. Acquire an interesting selection of serving dishes (see Equipment) and serve each recipe on a background that makes it look its best. Plain vegetables take on glamour against your most elaborate export china; even shapes can add variety: shrimp looks fine on a round plate or a shell-shaped platter; ribs are most at home on a long dish. Take a good look at your serving dishes and add to them if necessary.

(There are several schools of thought about the names of Chinese dishes. The dominant ones are 'flight of fancy" and "plain truth." This book has opted for the plain descriptive names, and those in English. Rendering Chinese names into the Roman alphabet is fraught with error, to say nothing of the errors introduced when the Cantonese version of a Szechuan name is further translated.)

Tea is the beverage we usually associate with Chinese food, but in China tea would not be served throughout the meal; it would instead be brought with rice as a light last course. Soup would be drunk with the food instead of tea. Hot spicy Szechuan food takes very well to cold beer or chilled, not-too-dry white wine. Please do not drown the meal in tea. The cold beer is a lot better!

There is no reason why you can't mix Szechuan dishes and Western dishes at a meal. Some very successful menus combine the things you like best from both cuisines. Don't be intimidated; you want to serve an enjoyable meal, not win a prize for authenticity. Several of the recipes in this book (see Index) make elegant and unusual first courses or hors d'oeuvres at any meal or party, though they are not traditionally served that way in China.

If your family and guests demand desserts, go ahead and serve them. There are not so many authentic Szechuan recipes, but there is no reason why you can't serve a Western favorite. Just keep in mind the other components of the meal and don't overwhelm with a huge rich dessert after a large meal. Light sweets are often served between the courses of a very elaborate Chinese dinner; you could use sherbet or fruit the same way. A familiar dessert that is very good as an interlude or at the end of a Szechuan meal is caramel custard, or flan. It is not an authentic recipe at all since milk is not used much in China, but it is light, not too sweet, and goes very well with the spicy foods.

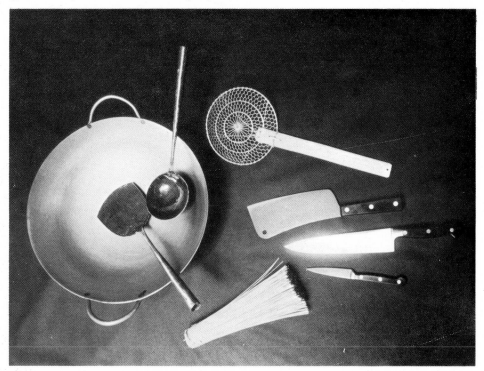

Basic Chinese cooking equipment: a 14" wok, cleaver, large and small knife, ladle, broad spatula, and strainer (very handy for retrieving food). The brush is a wok-scrubber.

Chinese vegetables

A WORD ABOUT ETIQUETTE

If you are fortunate enough to be invited to dinner with Chinese friends, you may find a few words about etiquette helpful. First, remember that age and hospitality are sacred. As a guest, you will be honored second only to elderly friends and relatives. Though we tend to think of people from the Orient as shy and reserved, your quiet but gracious admiration and appreciation of the occasion and surroundings will be very much in order, as will your respectful attention to older people present.

Usually, all the main dishes for a meal are put on the table at once. Help yourself to those near you and offer to serve the plates of those who cannot reach the dishes you can. If there is no serving spoon, use their chopsticks. They are not supposed to touch the mouth when you eat, so they are quite sanitary.

It is perfectly good form to lift your rice bowl from the table and hold it close to your mouth when eating from it. Indeed, it is almost impossible to eat rice with chopsticks without getting into range! Also, it is all right to take rather noisy sips of soup from the bowl; mixing air with the soup not only cools it but is supposed to develop its flavor. This is not to say that you have to slurp your soup if it doesn't come naturally to you, but you may not glare at those who do.

You probably wouldn't, anyway, but do not blow your nose noisily in company; it is considered an intensely private function, which, come to think of it, it is.

In the West you will probably find a napkin at your place. If there isn't a napkin, you will no doubt be given hot damp towels after any messy courses. If you think of it, a tissue in the pocket might be handy just as a fail safe.

A note expressing your pleasure in the dinner extended to you is always in good taste, as are flowers for your hostess. Send them, however; no lady, East or West, can cope with getting flowers in water, greeting guests, and serving a meal all at the same time!

Szechuan cooking is not difficult, and it is very rewarding for the effort it does require. I hope you will enjoy cooking and eating these recipes as much as I've enjoyed researching and testing them.

LOUISE STALLARD
New York, 1973

CHICKEN

CHICKEN

Chicken is very important in Szechuan cooking. In fact, it may be the most-used meat in the whole cuisine.

We are lucky to be living at a time when chickens are plentiful, relatively inexpensive, and tender. If you have forgotten how chickens used to be, just look at a cook book ten years old; the instructions for cooking chicken read like storming a fort. And with good reason: The purchaser could almost count on getting a fairly athletic bird unless it had been raised at home. If you are using a cherished old cookbook, by the way, you will have found that the cooking times given need to be drastically reduced for today's birds. On the other hand, it is now very hard to get a real stewing fowl. It is not clear what happens to old tasty chickens, but they do not come to rest in supermarkets. See if your good butcher can get hens for you; they make much better soup than young tender chickens.

The recipes in this section have been written for today's chickens and traditional Chinese accompaniments. Do not overcook the meat, especially when it is to be used by itself, as in Cold Chicken with Fresh Ginger and Garlic. If the chicken is dry and tasteless, the dish will be very disappointing. When the sliced or shredded meat is cooked, it should be removed from the heat as soon as it becomes opaque white. It will continue to cook from the heat in the dish, and if it is subjected to too much heat, it will shrink and become tough.

WHITE CUT CHICKEN
(Basic Stewed Chicken)

1 fowl, about 7 pounds (the older chicken will make a tastier dish)
7 cups water

You will need a large heavy pot with a tight lid to make this dish. It should not be too deep—you will want to retrieve the bird easily; a Dutch oven would be good.

Wash the chicken inside and out and put in the pot in *cold* water. Over high heat bring the pot to a rolling boil. Put on the cover and reduce the heat at once so that the water simmers. Check the chicken for tenderness after 1½ hours and every half hour thereafter. It should be tender but not coming apart. When it is done, remove the chicken from the broth and let it cool. Store it well wrapped in the refrigerator. Save the broth for cooking or to use as a delicious soup base.

White cut chicken can be eaten as it is, cut into small chunks, bones and all, and served with soy sauce. Meat from the chicken can also be used in all recipes that call for cooked chicken.

CHINESE ROAST CHICKEN

1 5-pound chicken (A capon would be excellent.)
   water to half cover chicken
1 cup soy sauce
2 tablespoons sugar
2 tablespoons sherry
1 piece fresh ginger about 1″ × ½″, minced
1 medium onion, diced

Wash chicken and truss it so it will hold its shape while cooking. Place the chicken in a heavy pan and add just enough water to come to its wings. Remove chicken and add the rest of the ingredients to the pot and bring to a boil. Return chicken to the pot and boil 15 minutes. Remove from heat and let stand at least 30 minutes.

Heat the oven to 500° F. Remove the chicken from cooking stock and dry thoroughly. Rub with just enough oil to moisten the breast and legs. Place the bird on a rack over a roasting pan and cook until completely browned, about 10 or 15 minutes. Allow bird to stand outside the oven 15 or 20 minutes to reabsorb juices if it is to be carved. Serve cooking stock, strained, separately, or thicken it with cornstarch to make gravy. Taste for seasonings.

Chinese Roast Chicken, first step (page 33)

CHICKEN IN A POT

 1 **stewing fowl, about 7 pounds (or 2 frying chickens)**
    water barely to cover
¾ **cup soy sauce**
¼ **cup sweet sherry**
 1 **piece fresh ginger about 1″ × ½″, sliced**
 1 **clove garlic, peeled and crushed**
 2 **teaspoons sugar**
 1 **large or 2 medium onions, roughly chopped**

Wash the bird inside and out and dry thoroughly with paper towels. Pull some of the fat from the inside of the chicken and render it over medium heat in a skillet large enough to hold the chicken. Truss and brown the bird on all sides, taking care not to let it cook too much—medium heat and patience work best here.

Place the browned chicken in a heavy pot and add water barely to cover. Bring to a rolling boil, then reduce heat so broth simmers. Add the other ingredients and cover the pot tightly. Cook gently until the chicken is tender when tested with a fork but not falling off the bones.

To serve, remove the chicken from the stock and let it cool. Cut it into bite-sized pieces and serve with reheated and reduced pot liquor.

If there is a lot of soup left, it can be used as sauce for other dishes or served suitably diluted with sliced dried mushrooms cooked in it. Very good.

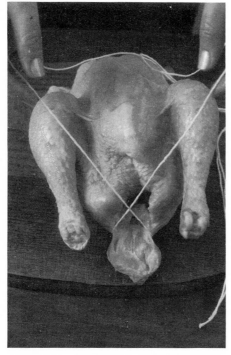

a

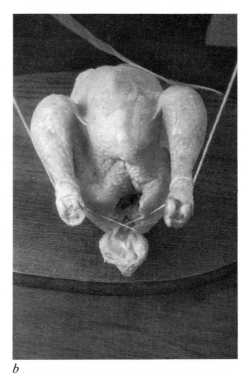

b

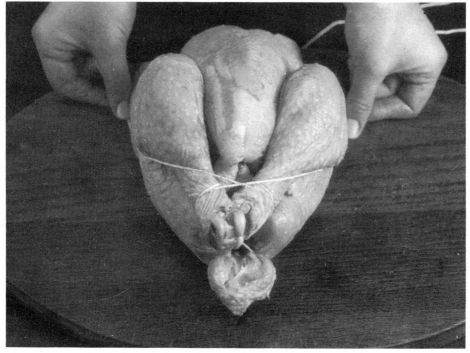

c

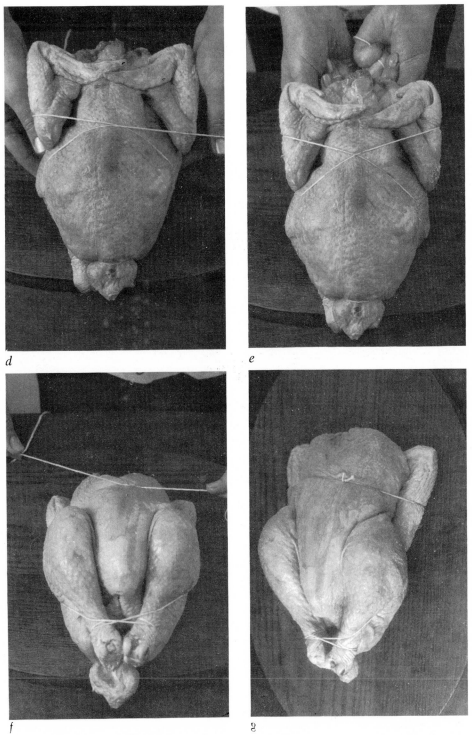

a) Place center of 4' string under the bird's tail and cross. b) Take string outside legs and wrap toward center. c) Cross string and draw around middle of legs toward chicken's back. d) Turn bird on its breast. Cross strings at mid-back. e) Take string around the wings (tips tucked behind). f) Tie strings tight over the breast. g) Cut off any excess string. The bird is ready to cook.

CHICKEN AND PEPPERS I

 2 whole chicken breasts, raw
 2 or more cloves garlic, peeled and minced
¼ cup soy sauce
¼ teaspoon pepper
 1 teaspoon sugar
 6 whole scallions or 1 medium onion
 1 green bell pepper
 1 red bell pepper
 1 small hot red fresh pepper

Skin and bone chicken breasts. Slice the meat into ¼″ slices, then into 1″ squares. Toss with just enough oil to coat, not more than 1 tablespoon. Add garlic, soy sauce, pepper, sugar; stir to mix thoroughly and let stand at least 15 minutes. (If preparations are made ahead, this part of the recipe could be kept in the refrigerator, tightly covered, overnight.)

Slice the scallions or finely dice the onion. Wash and seed the bell peppers and cut them into slivers. Wash and seed the hot pepper and mince finely. Measure 1 tablespoon* of hot pepper and set aside. Heat 3 tablespoons oil in a large skillet. Sauté the bell peppers until they are almost tender. Add the scallions or onion and cook 1 minute more. Lift chicken from marinade into skillet with a slotted spoon and cook just until the meat has turned white on both sides. Sprinkle hot pepper over chicken and sprinkle with additional soy sauce if the meat appeares to be drying too much. Heat and stir until the red pepper is heated through.

* Taste, for goodness' sake, and adjust amount to hotness of pepper.

CHICKEN AND PEPPERS II

An interesting variation of the above recipe uses the rest of the chickens and is very good with leftover turkey or duck as well.

Substitute the thighs and drumsticks from 2 3-pound chickens for the 2 whole breasts called for. Cut in slightly smaller squares (the nature of legs and thighs being what they are, you will probably have pieces more like slivers than squares; not to worry) and continue recipe as before. If leftover meat is used, let it marinate, but add it to the skillet only long enough to heat through. Do not let it cook again.

Turkey is especially tasty if chili pasilla is used as the hot pepper. It will come dried; soak it for 5 minutes or so in very hot water to soften. Slice down the middle and carefully remove the seeds —they are *very* hot. Add finely diced chili very cautiously until the dish is definitely hot but not painful.

A teaspoon of grated orange peel added to the duck version of this dish with the meat helps it a great deal. A dash of lemon or tart orange juice also helps cut the fat of leftover duck.

CHICKEN WITH WALNUTS

 2 whole raw breasts from frying chickens
½ teaspoon cornstarch
 1 tablespoon soy sauce
¼ teaspoon white pepper
¼ teaspoon sugar
 1 tablespoon oil
 1 cup walnuts
 1 thin slice ham, finely shredded

Skin and bone chicken and slice it very thin. Then cut slices into 1″ squares. Mix cornstarch, soy sauce, white pepper, sugar, and oil together and pour it over chicken. Stir to coat well. Plunge the walnuts into boiling water for a moment, then soak in cold water. Drain after 5 minutes and rub to remove husks.

Heat just enough oil in a skillet to cover the bottom. Add walnuts and sauté until just golden. Sprinkle with a little salt. Remove the walnuts from the pan and add a little more oil if necessary. Lift chicken squares from marinade with a slotted spoon and fry just until chicken is white on both sides. Return walnuts to the pan and heat just enough to warm through. Add ham, shredded, and remove from the heat at once. Before serving, sprinkle with a little soy sauce to taste.

CHICKEN VELVET

```
   2 whole raw breasts from frying chickens
   3 tablespoons water
1 ½ teaspoons cornstarch
   3 egg whites
   1 teaspoon salt
   ¼ teaspoon white pepper
   ½ cup unsalted chicken broth
   1 tablespoon soy sauce
   1 tablespoon sweet sherry
   ½ cup finely sliced ham or cured roast pork
```

Skin and bone chicken breasts and cut them into very fine shreds. A cleaver (or two cleavers) and a good chopping block are the fastest implements, but a sharp knife used to slice, then mince, then chop, will do. Sprinkle the chicken with a little water from the 3 tablespoons if it seems to dry out while you are cutting it.

When chicken is finely cut, mix the rest of the water, the cornstarch, egg whites, salt, and pepper and stir into the chicken. Heat a skillet over medium heat and grease it with a teaspoon of oil. Pour in enough of the chicken mixture to barely cover the bottom of the pan and cook gently, stirring and pushing with a spatula. When the chicken is just white, remove the batch from the pan and repeat cooking procedure. Use only enough oil to keep the chicken from sticking. Keep the already cooked batches on a warmed platter and serve as soon as all the chicken and the sauce are ready.

To make the sauce, combine chicken broth, soy sauce, and sherry. Bring to a boil and let reduce slightly. Stir in the ham or pork and pour over the chicken velvet.

This dish can be made also by beating two of the egg whites as for a soufflé and adding them to the chicken mixture. Then teaspoonfuls of the mixture are dropped into deep fat and cooked only until they are very pale brown. Whichever method is used, the chicken should be only just done and never overcooked.

Another delicious variation is adding ½ cup finely sliced and chopped white mushrooms to the chicken mixture before cooking. Canned mushrooms may be substituted, but fresh ones are better.

Crisp Roast Chicken (page 45)

CHICKEN WITH VEGETABLES

 2 whole raw breasts of chicken
 6 stalks of broccoli
12 tiny white carrots (these will be canned, probably)
    or 12 tiny Belgian carrots
 2 tablespoons oil
 2 teaspoons cornstarch
 1 teaspoon salt
½ teaspoon white pepper
¼ cup unsalted chicken broth or water

Skin and bone chicken breasts and cut meat into ½″ cubes. Wash and dry the broccoli and let drain for several hours. Cut each head into flowerlets about ½″ in diameter. (Use the stems for soup or another recipe, say Chicken Livers and Gizzards with Vegetables.) Drain the carrots and dry them with paper towels. If tiny carrots are not available, a good substitute would be similar amounts of sweet (nonhot) white radishes or celery root.

When ready to cook and serve, heat the oil in a skillet. Keep heat medium. Sauté without browning the chicken on both sides. It should just turn opaque white. When you turn the chicken, add the broccoli flowerets to the skillet, stirring to coat them with oil. Reduce heat as much as possible, cover the pan, and cook for 3 minutes. Test the broccoli; it should be crisp-tender and still bright green. Mix the rest of the ingredients and pour into the pan. Increase heat slightly and cook, stirring carefully, just until sauce is thickened and coats chicken and broccoli. Very carefully stir in carrots and just heat through.

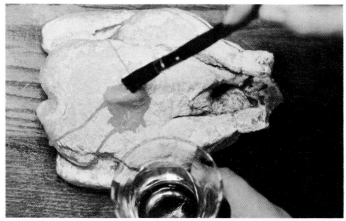

a

b

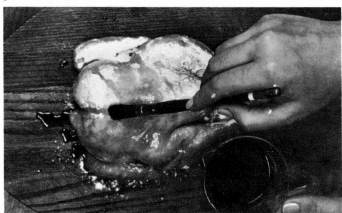

c

Preparation of Crisp Roast Chicken

a) Baste and flour steamed chicken; let dry, then baste again.
b) Sift flour generously over basted chicken. c) Continue
flouring and basting, letting dry, until flour and basting
liquid are used up.

CRISP ROAST CHICKEN

 1 **whole roasting chicken, about 4 pounds**
 ¼ **cup soy sauce**
 ¼ **cup lemon juice or rice wine vinegar**
 ½ **cup honey or currant jelly**
 ¼ **cup sherry**
 ½ **cup flour**

Clean and wash the chicken and truss it so it will hold its shape during cooking. Place on a rack above 2 inches of water and steam, covered, until bird is almost tender. (Check after 30 minutes and often thereafter.)

Remove the chicken from the steamer and put it immediately into the freezer (or the coolest part of the refrigerator) for 15 minutes. Remove it and dry with paper towels. Mix together soy sauce, lemon juice, honey, and sherry. Brush the bird all over with liquid, then sift flour over it. Let dry. Repeat until basting liquid and flour are gone (usually 3 times, but you may be a more economical brusher and/or sifter).

Heat the oven to full blast (550° F. on most ranges). Brush the bird with oil or very, very soft margarine, being very careful not to disturb the crust created by basting and dusting. Place the chicken on a rack over a pan and put it in the oven. Watch it like a hawk; you want a beautiful golden crisp crust, not cinders.

The steamed chicken can also be cut up, basted and dusted, and then deep-fried, or you might want to try frying the bird whole. Getting the coated, trussed chicken into and out of the hot (375° F.) deep fat is more than your correspondent cares to face, however.

Duck is very good this way, too, but a few adjustments in the method are necessary. See Crisp Roast Duck.

KUNG PAO CHICKEN

  breast and thighs from 3-pound frying chicken
8 dried black mushrooms
2 chilis serranos or other small hot green chilis
4 water chestnuts or ¼ cup bamboo shoots (canned chunks)
½ cup blanched almonds
2 tablespoons oil
2 cloves garlic, minced
2 tablespoons soy sauce
¼ teaspoon dry mustard
½ teaspoon sugar
¼ teaspoon ground dry ginger
½ cup blanched French-cut green beans or raw snow peas

Skin and bone the chicken. Cut meat in ½″ cubes. Soak mushrooms in very hot water for 5 minutes; drain and dry, then cut in thin slices. Remove the seeds from the chilis and discard. Slice the chilis into very thin slices. Drain water chestnuts or bamboo shoots. Slice water chestnuts into thirds or chop bamboo into ¼″ cubes. Toast almonds in a moderate oven or brown in a little oil in a small frying pan.

To cook the dish, heat oil in a heavy skillet. Add thigh meat of chicken first. Sauté on one side, then add breast meat. (The breast takes just half as long to cook as the thigh.) Chicken should not brown much but just cook through. Remove chicken when it is opaque and add garlic to the skillet. Cook 1 minute, then add chilis.

Mix the rest of the ingredients except the beans or peas. Return chicken to skillet and add almonds. Pour the soy sauce mixture over all and stir over high heat until sauce is slightly thickened and coats meat well. Add the green beans or snow peas and reduce heat at once. Cover tightly and cook 3 minutes. Check beans or peas. They should be just barely tender and still bright green. Serve at once.

N.B. If you do not have a favorite way of blanching beans, you might try putting them in a wire strainer and lowering that into a big pot of boiling water for *one* minute. Remove at once and let them drain, stirring so that all will cool quickly.

CHICKEN LIVERS WITH TREE EARS AND SCALLIONS

½ pound chicken livers
10 dried black Chinese mushrooms (or Italian mushrooms, dried)
 6 to 10 scallions, depending on the size
 1 tablespoon oil
¼ cup sherry
 2 tablespoons soy sauce
 1 teaspoon lemon juice or rice wine vinegar
   black pepper to taste

Drain and dry chicken livers. Soak mushrooms for 5 minutes in very hot water. Clean scallions and slice in ½" pieces (cut diagonally), green and all.

Heat oil in a skillet. Drain and dry mushrooms and slice them in ¼" slices. Cook just until tender, then push to one side of pan. Sauté the chicken livers and scallions together; turn the livers once so that both sides cook evenly.

When livers are just done, remove to serving dish. Mix sherry and soy sauce and pour into skillet with mushrooms and scallions. Stir to get up all the good bits that will stick to the skillet. Add lemon juice and pour sauce over livers. Serve at once. Pass the pepper grinder at the table.

N.B. Sweet vermouth is also very good in this recipe. And another variation is dry vermouth—also good with beef liver.

CHICKEN HEARTS AND GIZZARDS WITH VEGETABLES

½ pound chicken hearts or gizzards or a mixture of both
 1 cup thinly sliced white vegetable
½ cup thinly sliced dark green vegetable
 2 tablespoons oil
 2 tablespoons soy sauce
 2 teaspoons dry mustard
 1 teaspoon sugar

Wash and dry chicken hearts. Wash gizzards and place in a saucepan. Barely cover with cold water and bring to a boil. Reduce heat so that broth simmers and cover pan. Poach until gizzards are almost tender. (A sharp knife should pierce them easily.) Remove gizzards and drain. When they are cool enough to handle, remove the tough whitish membrane—you will have two small pieces of meat from each gizzard. Cut each piece in half and slice each raw chicken heart in half lengthwise.

Prepare vegetables by peeling off tough outer skin (such as that on broccoli stems), then slicing thin. Cabbage, the hard center of bok choy (Chinese celery), celery, or bamboo shoots might be the light-colored vegetable; broccoli, spinach (in which case shred instead of slice), watercress, or string beans would make a pretty contrast.

Heat the oil in a large skillet. Add the dry chicken giblets and stir and cook quickly. Add the vegetables and just sprinkle with water. When vegetables are crisp-tender, remove from heat. Mix soy sauce, mustard, and sugar and pour over meat and vegetables.

Chicken Gizzards with Peppers and Spinach

CHICKEN GIZZARDS WITH PEPPERS AND SPINACH

½ pound chicken gizzards
1 6″ chili pasilla
½ pound raw spinach
2 tablespoons oil
2 tablespoons soy sauce
½ teaspoon dry mustard

Wash and dry gizzards; remove tough membrane from each one so that two small spheres of meat are left. Slice each sphere into two pieces. Soak the chili pasilla in very hot water for 10 minutes. Drain and dry and slice in ¼″ slices. Remove and discard all the seeds. Wash and drain the spinach and remove any tough stems. Shred the leaves into ½″ pieces.

Heat the oil in a skillet. Add the gizzards and sauté until they are tender. Add the chili pasilla and stir so that it cooks on all sides. Meanwhile, mix the soy sauce and dry mustard. Add the spinach to the skillet, pour the soy sauce mixture over it, and tightly cover the pan. Reduce the heat at once and cook for 5 minutes. When the dish is ready to serve, the spinach should be wilted but still bright green. Stir the skillet well before placing the dish on a serving platter.

CHICKEN LIVERS WITH BAMBOO SHOOTS

½ pound chicken livers
1 cup bamboo shoots (canned are fine)
1 tablespoon oil or lard (lard is better)
  tiny pinch cinnamon
1 tablespoon orange marmalade or fruit liqueur

Drain and dry chicken livers. Drain bamboo shoots. Heat oil or lard in a skillet and sauté livers on both sides. Keep heat gentle and watch carefully so that they don't overcook. Add bamboo shoots and stir just to heat through. Sprinkle with cinnamon and add marmalade or liqueur. Cook and stir just enough to coat livers and bamboo shoots with the sauce. Serve soy sauce to add to taste.

QUICK POACHED CHICKEN

1 frying chicken, about 3 pounds
6 cups water

Put the water into a heavy pot with a tight-fitting lid and bring it to a boil. Meanwhile, wash the chicken. When water is boiling, put the chicken into the pot. Cover immediately and reduce heat so that the broth simmers. Check for tenderness after 15 minutes and very frequently thereafter; the bird should be done in a very short time. (It will cook even quicker if it is allowed to warm up from the refrigerator before cooking.)

Poached frying chicken can be used for any recipes calling for cooked chicken, and it is especially delicate in dishes with light, subtle sauces.

The broth is good for cooking and is easy to clarify; it makes an elegant base for your most ambitious soups.

HUNG CHICKEN

This is not a Chinese name; the bird is actually hung up to cure. To do it successfully, you will need a place to hang the chicken, say an outside porch or very cool pantry where the air can circulate freely. A smokehouse would be just the thing. You will also need some time, patience, and quite cold, but not hard-freezing, weather.

First, buy a young tender chicken about 5 to 7 pounds in weight. You could cure a smaller bird, but it would hardly be worth the trouble. Have the poultry man kill it but ask that he clean it only by removing the insides through as small a slit as possible under the wing. Or you can do it yourself. Dry the inside of the bird thoroughly with paper towels. Now you have a dry empty bird with its head, feet, and feathers *on*.

Heat a skillet and in it combine about ¼ cup coarse salt and 1 teaspoon ground Szechuan peppercorns. Stir and cook until the mixture is very hot. Let it cool enough to handle, then rub it into the inside of the chicken well. Do not stint. Now, tuck the bird's head under one wing and tie lightly if necessary to keep it there. Knot stout cord around the feet and hoist away. It should hang for 10 days at the absolute minimum; 2 weeks or 3 would be better. It will keep for up to 10 weeks before cooking, but that would seem to be pushing good luck.

To cook, heat a big pot of water to boiling. Remove it from the heat and let the bubbling stop. Take down the chicken and plunge it into the scalding water. The feathers should then come off easily. Watch the water temperature; if it is too cool, the feathers won't come off easily. If it is too hot, the skin will cook and the feathers won't come off easily, either; furthermore, a lot of skin will be torn. Better pluck the chicken outdoors; it gets a bit messy in the best of times. Take off the head and the feet. (Save feet for soup.) Put the plucked chicken in a kettle with boiling water just to cover. Cook 15 minutes and test. It should be very tender. Serve hot or cold. Use the soup, too.

COLD HACKED CHICKEN WITH WARM SWEET SAUCE

 1 2½- to 3-pound frying chicken
½ cup unsalted chicken stock or water
 1 tablespoon soy sauce
¼ cup sweet sherry
¼ teaspoon salt
    pinch freshly grated dry ginger
 3 chilis pequines
 2 tablespoons oil

Poach the chicken in water barely to cover. Do not add salt and do not overcook. Cool in broth.

To make sauce, combine the rest of the ingredients except the chilis and oil in a saucepan and bring to a boil. Reduce heat to simmering and cook uncovered until mixture is reduced to a scant ½ cup. Meanwhile, in a skillet, toast the chilis in the oil. The chilis should be dark brown, but do not let them burn. Be careful not to inhale too much of the aroma that rises while the chilis cook—it is *very* hot. Remove the skillet from heat and add sauce. If you like hot sauce, crush the toasted chilis with a large spoon and leave them in; if you prefer a milder version, fish them out and discard.

When ready to serve, drain and dry the chicken. Remove the joints at the end of drumsticks, backbone, and wing tips and cut into bite-sized pieces, bones and all. A cleaver is the most efficient implement to use, but it takes a strong chopping block and a measure of brio; a heavy knife and a mallet are the coward's way out. However you accomplish it, arrange the cut chicken on a serving dish and pour sauce over it. Serve the cold chicken with the warm sauce at once.

N.B. Hacked chicken is tasty served with drinks but a little messy. Toothpicks are not enough. Provide plates, small forks or chopsticks, and plenty of napkins.

COLD CHICKEN WITH FRESH GINGER AND GARLIC

breast and thighs from one chicken (a fryer about 3 pounds) or a similar
amount of leftover cooked chicken
¾ cups unsalted chicken stock or water
2 tablespoons soy sauce
¼ teaspoon dry mustard
½ teaspoon sugar
fresh ginger to taste*
2 or more cloves of garlic, peeled
2 cucumbers, sliced
1 whole scallion or sprigs of fresh chives

Both the chicken and the sauce for this dish need to be cooked, then thoroughly cooled, so start preparations early on the day it is to be served or, better yet, the day before.

Poach the chicken in about 3 cups unsalted water. Do not over-cook; it should be tender but not falling off the bones. Let it cool completely in the stock. If it is to be kept more than the time it takes to cool, store in the refrigerator.

To make the sauce, take enough stock from the chicken pot to give ¾ cup after all the fat is skimmed off. (Or use water; canned stock or broth made from bouillon cubes is too salty and combined with the soy sauce will make a briny sauce.) In a blender combine the stock, soy sauce, mustard, sugar, ginger, and garlic. Blend until the mixture is smooth. If you do not have a blender, cut up the garlic and ginger and pound in a mortar with a pestle until smooth and add to liquids.

Pour into a saucepan and bring to a boil. Reduce heat so that the sauce simmers and cook uncovered until it is about the consistency of thin hollandaise. This will take some little time if the pan is small and deep; a larger, flatter pan will need careful watching to make sure the liquid doesn't boil away entirely! When the sauce is thickened, store in a tightly covered jar to cool thoroughly. Store in the refrigerator.

To serve, remove the chicken from the stock and dry it thoroughly. (Paper towels are handy.) Slice into thin long pieces and arrange on a serving dish. Save the most beautiful slices for the top of the mound. This is not dishonesty, just tact. Put slices of cucumbers around the chicken and pour the cold sauce over the chicken. Sprinkle the sauce with thin slices of scallion or snips of chives.

Both the chicken and the sauce should be cool but not icy. Let them moderate a bit if they have been stored in the refrigerator.

N.B. This dish makes a fine hors d'oeuvre, too. Cut the chicken in cubes instead of thin slices and impale each cube on a tooth-pick. The sauce is better poured over all at the beginning than used for a dip; it is a little intense as a dip.

---

* Start with a piece of ginger about 1″ long and ½″ in diameter and then taste. You will probably want to add 3 pieces this size or its equivalent in all; the sauce is *supposed* to be hot.

Cold Chicken in Red Hot Oil

COLD CHICKEN IN RED HOT OIL

breast and thighs from one frying chicken
1 cup peanut or sesame oil
3 dried hot red peppers, whole, or 1 chili pasilla about 6 inches long, or 6 chilis pequines

Poach the chicken pieces in unsalted water and cool in the stock. Store in the refrigerator until ready to serve.

Bring oil and chilis you are using (each variety will give a slightly different taste, but each is good) to smoking hot in a small saucepan. Remove from the heat and let cool. Pour into a jar with a tight-fitting lid and store at room temperature until ready to use, but at least 12 hours. The flavor and color of the oil will develop for 4 days or so. Then it should be stored in the refrigerator. It will continue to get hotter as long as the chilis are left in it. You may want to taste it after the first 12 hours and decide if you want to defuse it then.

To serve, cut the chicken meat into long thin bite-sized slices and toss with just enough oil to coat. You will probably have oil left over, but 1 cup is the best quantity to make; smaller amounts of oil burn while heating. Pass the soy sauce or coarse salt at the table.

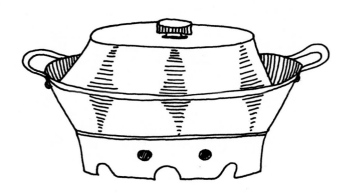

CHINESE-STYLE TURKEY

Turkey is not a bird used in China, but roasted this way it is very good and a bit of a change from the usual stuffed holiday turkey.

1 **turkey, about 18 pounds,** *not* **prebasted or stuffed**
3 **quarts water**
3 **cups soy sauce**
1 ½ **cups sherry**
¼ **cup dark brown sugar**
1 **piece fresh ginger about 2″ × ½″**
1 **large onion, quartered**
1 **tablespoon salt**

Wash the turkey inside and out and truss so it will hold its shape during cooking. Make cooking stock by boiling the rest of the ingredients together for 15 minutes. Add the turkey to the pot and simmer 15 minutes on each side, about 1½ hours in all, turning to make sure all parts of the bird get into the stock.

Remove turkey from pot and drain. Heat the oven very hot, 500° F., and place turkey over a roasting pan in a rack, breast down. Roast 30 minutes, basting once with 1 cup water. Turn bird on its back and roast 30 minutes more, basting twice. Turn once more if sides need more browning. When done, remove from oven and let stand for 20 minutes before carving so the juices can settle.

DUCK

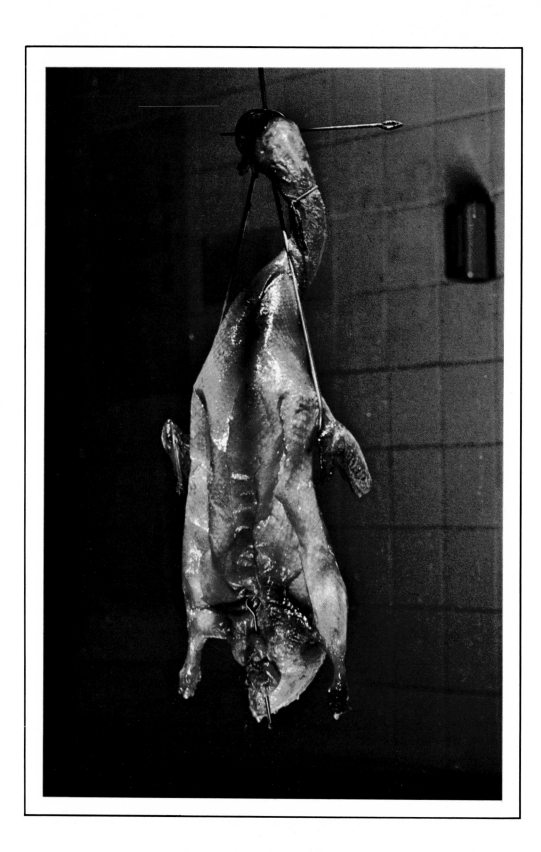

DUCK

Duck is not only very good, it is usually plentiful frozen. It is genuinely authentic Chinese food, too. The varieties are somewhat different here, but they lend themselves to Szechuan cooking methods splendidly.

Since most ducks available in supermarkets are frozen, let us pronounce a general plan for preparing them for cooking. First, let them thaw completely according to package instructions. If there aren't any instructions, plan to leave the bird in the refrigerator, not the freezer, for at least 24 hours before using. If it is not thoroughly thawed in that time, it can finish at room temperature. Check to make sure that the oil sack just above the tail has been removed. It usually will have been in commercially frozen ducks, but better safe than sorry. If there are any pin feathers, remove with tweezers. Remove the giblets if your duck has them; they make good broth but usually will not be needed as meat in these recipes.

If your duck is freshly killed, gut it as soon as you get it, or even better, train the hunter in your family to gut it in the field. If you provide him with a little bag of salt, perhaps he can also salt the inside before putting it in his bag. Ducks and game birds of all kinds hung with the entrails in are popular in some places, but the taste (politely called "gamey") seems to me acquired. Besides, ducks are too hard to shoot to take the chance of losing them to spoilage.

A freshly killed duck should be plucked after dipping it into water that has boiled but has been removed from the heat and allowed to stop bubbling. (See instructions for Hung Chicken.) Remove head and feet and oil sack above the tail. If the duck is to be used whole, examine the wing tips; if they are without meat, consider chopping them off and using them for soup. The finished bird will look better, and the oily, meatless wing tips will not be missed!

Wash and dry the bird thoroughly inside and out. Naturally, you don't have to be so careful about the drying if it is to be boiled.

Basic Duck

BASIC DUCK
(Red Cooked Duck)

1 **duck, about 6 pounds**
½ **cup soy sauce**
¼ **cup sweet sherry**
2 **scallions or 1 medium onion, sliced**

Leave the duck whole or cut it into serving pieces. Place in a pan with a tight-fitting lid and half cover it with cold water. Bring the liquid to a boil, then add the rest of the ingredients. Cook briskly for 10 minutes, then reduce heat to simmering and cover pan. Check for tenderness in 45 minutes. Duck should be quite tender and slightly drawing away from its bones. A whole duck will take longer than a cut-up one, of course.

Duck is usually served hot. The basic dish would be the cooked duck cut into bite-sized pieces and served with the cooking liquid, skimmed of all fat, thickened with a little cornstarch or not, as you please. Unthickened broth is more authentic and probably better for you!

Ingredients for Roast Duck Szechuan Style

ROAST DUCK SZECHUAN STYLE

1 6-pound duck
boiling water just to cover duck
½ cup soy sauce
¼ cup sherry
2 small onions, each stuck with 1 whole clove

Rinse and dry the duck. Truss it so it will hold its shape while cooking if you plan to serve it whole.

Place the duck in a large deep pan with a tight lid. Add boiling water just to cover and the rest of the ingredients. Bring to a boil, cover and reduce heat so pot simmers smartly. Cook 15 minutes; turn the duck and cook another 15 minutes. Let the duck cool in the sauce.

When ready to roast the duck (it can be kept in the refrigerator up to two weeks and in the freezer up to two months between poaching and roasting), heat the oven to 450° F. and prepare a basting sauce:

¼ cup soy sauce
2 tablespoons honey
1 teaspoon Szechuan peppercorns, ground
½ teaspoon ground cinnamon

Place the duck on a rack above a roasting pan and place in the oven. After 5 minutes baste all over with the soy-honey mixture. Roast 45 minutes in all, turning and basting every 15 minutes. (Add some boiling water to the roasting pan if the basting liquid begins to burn.) Serve at once.

PEPPER-BASTED ROAST DUCK

1 cup honey
1 cup brown sugar
1 ½ tablespoons ground Szechuan pepper
2 cloves garlic
1 piece fresh ginger about 3″ × ½″
¼ cup soy sauce
1 duck, about 6 pounds

Place the honey, brown sugar, ½ tablespoon of the Szechuan pepper, the garlic, sliced, the ginger, sliced, and the soy sauce in a blender. Process until the syrup is smooth. Pour into a saucepan and cook until it reaches 235° F. on a candy thermometer (soft-ball stage.)

Meanwhile, wash and dry the duck very well. Rub inside and out with the remaining tablespoon of Szechuan pepper combined with about 1 teaspoon salt. Truss so it will hold its shape. Place the duck on a rack above a roasting pan. Heat the oven to 450° F. Brush the duck with the syrup and cook until it is brown, about 10 minutes. Baste twice during browning. (Keep syrup over hot water in a double boiler.) Reduce the oven heat to 325° F. and continue roasting and basting (every 15 minutes) until duck is very tender, about 2 hours. As basting syrup collects in the roasting pan, add boiling water so it doesn't burn. A good rule of thumb is ½ cup boiling water each time the bird is basted, then as necessary. When duck is done, cut into serving pieces and serve hot. Skim fat from pan juices (if they haven't burned—in which case discard) and pass separately.

MARINATED FRIED DUCK

  breast and legs from a 6-pound duck
1 **tablespoon soy sauce**
1 **teaspoon salt**
¼ **cup sweet sherry**
1 **medium onion, thinly sliced**
1 **piece fresh ginger about 1″ × ½″, sliced or minced**
2 **egg yolks or 1 whole egg, slightly beaten**
½ **cup cornstarch**
¼ **cup lard or oil (lard is better)**

Wash duck; leave skin on. Split the breast and divide legs into thighs and drumsticks.

Mix soy sauce, salt, sherry, onion, and ginger together and marinate the duck at least 1 hour. (Overnight in the refrigerator would be even better.)

When ready to cook, drain and dry the duck pieces. Mix together the eggs, ¼ cup water, and enough cornstarch to give a thick paste. Spread over one side of the duck pieces and let dry 10 minutes; turn and repeat. (Put the battered side of the duck on a plate or piece of waxed paper sprinkled with the rest of the cornstarch so it won't stick or be disturbed.) Heat the lard in a skillet. When it is smoking hot, add the duck. Do not crowd—use a pan big enough to hold all the pieces easily or do it in two batches. Turn after 2 minutes and immediately reduce the heat. Turn again after another 2 minutes and cook until duck is very tender, turning once again, about 10 minutes on each side. Cut into bite-sized serving pieces and make sure that each person gets some breast and some leg meat. Pass the pepper grinder at the table.

Ingredients for Duck and Ginger Shreds

DUCK AND GINGER SHREDS

  breast and thighs from 1 6-pound duck
  1 piece of fresh ginger about 2″ × ½″*
  2 tablespoons soy sauce
  2 tablespoons sherry
  ½ teaspoon sugar
  2 teaspoons cornstarch
  3 tablespoons chopped scallion or onion
1 ½ tablespoons lard or oil

Wash and dry the duck and cut the meat into shreds. Cut the ginger into thin shreds and set aside. Toss the shredded duck with the soy sauce, sherry, sugar, cornstarch, and scallions. Let stand while lard heats in a skillet. When the fat is very hot, add the duck and marinade; stir to coat with oil and cook for 1 minute. Add the ginger and cook another 2 or 3 minutes, stirring constantly. Serve at once hot—this is one dish that does *not* improve with standing!

* If fresh ginger is not available, dried mushrooms (reconstituted) or hot or mild peppers could be substituted.

Roast ducks for sale in New York's Chinatown

CRISP ROAST DUCK

1 **duck, about 6 pounds**
¼ **cup soy sauce**
½ **cup lemon juice or rice wine vinegar**
2 **tablespoons honey**
2 **tablespoons brown sugar**
1 **teaspoon salt**

Clean and wash the duck and dry it. Truss if it is to be served whole. Cut it into serving pieces otherwise. (The smaller pieces are easier to handle.) Place the duck on the rack of a steamer and steam until the meat is fork-tender; check in 35 minutes and often thereafter. When it is done, remove from steamer and dry well. Place in the refrigerator until it is very cold. (Using the freezer will speed this step up somewhat, but allow enough time for the duck to get *cold*.)

About an hour before cooking, remove duck from the refrigerator. Mix the rest of the ingredients together and brush well over the duck. Let dry 10 minutes or so, then brush again. Repeat as long as there is time and liquid left. To cook, heat the oven to 550° F. Place the glazed duck on a rack over a roasting pan and place in the oven. Do not add oil—the duck will still have plenty in its skin to baste itself. Watch the duck carefully; it will be done when the skin is very crisp and quite dark. Don't let it burn, though; it will go from very dark brown (just right) to black (burned) fast indeed.

Braised Duck with Onion Stuffing

DUCK BRAISED WITH ONION STUFFING

1 **duck, about 6 pounds**
   enough scallions or onions to stuff duck snugly
2 **tablespoons soy sauce**
1 **tablespoon sugar**

Wash and dry the duck thoroughly for this recipe. Chop the scallions or onions roughly and stuff the duck. Truss the bird so it will keep its shape while cooking.

In a heavy pot with a tight-fitting lid, brown the duck on all sides over a brisk flame. If you control the heat and have patience, no extra shortening should be necessary; enough will cook out of the duck as it heats to brown it nicely. When it is browned, add to the pot:

   enough water to half cover the duck
¼ **cup sweet sherry**
1 **piece fresh ginger about 1″ × ½″, sliced thin**
¼ **cup soy sauce**

Bring to boiling, then reduce heat and cover tightly. Check after 45 minutes of simmering; the duck should be very tender.

To serve, drain the duck and cut into bite-sized pieces. Discard the onion; it has served its purpose. Skim fat from the cooking broth and pass separately.

SMOKED SZECHUAN DUCK

To smoke a duck, you will need a very, very well-ventilated kitchen. An outside porch or a back-yard grill would be even better. You will also need:

1 **peck hardwood chips and small pieces (Camphor wood would be used by Chinese people if they could get it; substitutes could be hickory, oak, or other hardwoods.)**
½ **cup tea leaves**
1 **duck, about 7 pounds**
¼ **cup salt**
2 **tablespoons saltpeter**
1 **tablespoon Szechuan peppercorns**

Prepare the fire bed (or pan of grill by arranging the wood over it). If the wood is very dry, sprinkle it with a little water to retard burning and give more smoke. Be sure that the rack on which the duck will rest is high enough above the fire bed so that the bird will smoke instead of roast.

Wash and dry the duck thoroughly. Rub it well inside with a mixture of salt, saltpeter, and crushed Szechuan peppercorns.

Start the wood burning. Sprinkle with more water if it flames up. Sprinkle about a tablespoon of the tea over the wood. Place the duck on the rack, put the rack over the fire, and cover rack, bird and all, with the dome of the smoker or a tent of foil or canvas. Smoke for about 20 minutes, turning the duck twice. Add tea leaves every few minutes until they are used up.

When the duck is smoked, hang it for at least six hours to let the flavors settle. To cook, steam until almost tender, then sauté. The bird is easier to handle if it is cut into serving pieces before sautéing; it can be cut into bite-sized pieces before serving. If the whole duck is to be served, after steaming, truss it so it will hold its shape. Brush with a mixture of ¼ cup soy sauce, 1 tablespoon lard, melted, and 2 tablespoons honey. Place in a 550° F. oven only until it is crisp, about 10 minutes. Baste often to make a crisp crust.

HOT MARINATED FRIED DUCK

    breast and legs from a 6-pound duck
1 **tablespoon soy sauce**
1 **teaspoon salt**
¼ **cup sweet sherry**
1 **medium onion, thinly sliced**
2 **cloves garlic, minced**
2 **chilis serranos or Italian hot green peppers**
1 **piece fresh ginger about 1″ × ½″, sliced or minced**
2 **egg yolks or 1 whole egg, slightly beaten**
½ **cup cornstarch**
¼ **cup lard or oil (Lard is better.)**

Wash duck; leave skin on. Split the breast and divide legs into thighs and drumsticks.

Mix soy sauce, salt, sherry, onion, peppers, and ginger together and marinate the duck overnight in the refrigerator.

To cook, drain and dry the duck pieces. Mix together the eggs, ¼ cup water, and enough cornstarch to give a thick paste. Spread over one side of the duck pieces and let dry 10 minutes; turn and repeat. (Put the battered side of the duck on a plate or piece of waxed paper sprinkled with the rest of the cornstarch so it won't stick or be disturbed.) Heat the lard in a skillet. When it is smoking hot, add the duck. Do not crowd; do it in several batches if necessary. Turn after 2 minutes and immediately reduce the heat. Turn again after 4 minutes and cook until duck is very tender, turning once again; allow about 10 minutes on each side. Cut into bite-sized serving pieces and make sure that each person gets some breast and some leg meat. Pass the pepper grinder at the table.

SHAN SU DUCK

Follow directions in Smoked Szechuan Duck for smoking bird. When that is done, rub the bird inside and out with:

1 tablespoon freshly ground black pepper
1 tablespoon freshly ground Szechuan pepper
6 whole scallions, minced

Stuff the smoked duck with 6 more whole scallions (or a medium onion), roughly sliced. Hang for 6 hours, then steam and sauté or glaze as for Szechuan Duck.

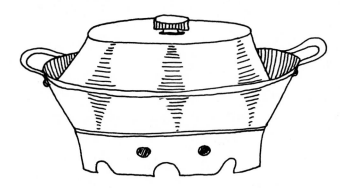

FISH
&
SEAFOOD

FISH
&
SEAFOOD

If this chapter had been titled "Seafood" alone, it would have been very short indeed: there isn't any seafood in Szechuan! An inland province, it traditionally had no fish from the sea at all. Though modern transportation and refrigeration have made seafoods available in the interior, the classic cuisine does not include them. Some are very good prepared Szechuan *style,* however, and those recipes are included in this section.

Freshwater fish abounds, and delicate freshwater shrimp are widely used. Carp, bass, perch, and other white-fleshed fish widely available here are also used in China. Also, in most recipes saltwater fish may be substituted without sacrificing anything but authenticity. If Chinese dried shrimp are available, they are excellent for the shrimp dishes; simply soak them in hot water to barely cover for 10 or 15 minutes (or according to the package directions).

In general, fish for Szechuan dishes is prepared for cooking by gutting and washing well; the head and tail are left *on*. The flavor is better, and keeping the fish intact helps hold it together. The bones, fins, head, and tail come off easily when the fish is cooked. Since the meat and the taste are delicate, sauces are usually subtle, also.

Most important, fish should not be overcooked. When it "flakes," the usual instruction given in Western cooking, it is already too done to be served at its best. Careful watching, which is necessary to cook fish successfully, is not difficult since the whole process takes so little time. For most fish dishes you should have your guests at the table and busy on another course before you begin cooking the fish. They can wait a bit, but the fish won't!

Although it is true that there was not any seafood in Szechuan in years past, this is not to say that the taste of seafood was not prized. It surely was, to the extent that the resourceful cooks devised a flavoring sauce to impart "fish flavor" to other meats, most especially pork (highly prized) and chicken. The sauce is made of garlic, scallions, ginger, fermented rice wine, and hot peppers to taste, and it does make meat taste like fish. The proportions are a little elusive since they vary with the strength of the individual ingredients, especially the wine, and the resistance to fishiness the meat to be treated offers. Whether you would like to experiment with "fish flavor" and whether it seems, in this day of well-stocked supermarkets, a good idea, I leave to you.

PLAIN STEAMED FISH

1 **2-pound white-fleshed fish**
1 **tablespoon soy sauce**
1 **tablespoon sherry**
1 **piece of fresh ginger about 1″ × ½″ (optional)**
1 **slice onion**
   water barely to cover fish

To steam a fish, it is necessary to have a steamer that will hold both the fish and its interior pan. A large double boiler will do, or better yet a clam steamer or some other pot of that size with a rack to hold the interior pan and the fish. If the fish is a close fit, skewer it and bend it a bit. (This will give a faint appearance of swimming if your imagination is very good.) The bending may make it fit.

Clean and dry the whole fish. Mix the soy sauce, sherry, ginger, and onion in the interior bowl or pan or the top of the double boiler. Place the fish in the interior bowl and add just enough hot water to cover it. Place the bowl in the steamer (or over the bottom of the double boiler), which has 2″ of water boiling in it. Cover tightly and steam until the fish is barely cooked, 145° F. on a meat thermometer inserted in the thickest part of the flesh, about 15 minutes. Check often as steaming time comes to an end. Do not overcook the fish. Serve at once; pass the soy sauce. (New soy sauce, that is—the cooking liquid has served its purpose.)

SHRIMP WITH VEGETABLES

½ **pound fresh raw shrimp**
1 **cup broccoli flowerets**
12 **tiny white carrots or ½ cup bamboo shoots or water chestnuts or thinly sliced hearts of bok choy**
1 **teaspoon oil**
½ **cup unsalted chicken broth or water**
2 **teaspoons cornstarch**
1 **teaspoon salt**
½ **teaspoon white pepper**

Wash and shell the shrimp. Wash and thoroughly dry the broccoli. Drain the carrots (they come canned) and dry with paper towels.

Heat oil in a skillet. Add broccoli and toss to coat thoroughly. Cook 1 minute over medium heat. Add chicken broth just to cover the bottom of the skillet. Cover tightly and cook 2 minutes. Check broccoli; it should be barely tender and still bright green. (If bok choy or other raw vegetable is used, add it at the same time the broccoli is put in the skillet and increase the oil to 2 teaspoons.) Add the shrimp to the skillet and again add just enough broth to keep pan moist. Cover and cook 1 minute. The shrimp should be barely opaque. While the shrimp cooks, mix cornstarch with salt, pepper, and the remaining broth. When shrimp is barely done, pour sauce mixture into pan and stir briskly until it is thickened and coats shrimp and vegetables. Add carrots just to heat through and take on a coating of sauce. Serve at once.

SHRIMP WITH CASHEWS

½ pound fairly small raw shrimp*
½ pound unsalted cashews†
 1 teaspoon peanut oil
 1 teaspoon cornstarch or rice starch
    pinch freshly ground dried ginger root

Shell and clean the shrimp; set aside.

Place the cashews in a saucepan and barely cover them with water. Bring to a boil. Immediately remove the nuts with a slotted spoon and place in a colander to drain. Cover with a towel to keep warm. Put the shrimp into the boiling water and turn the heat off *at once*. Cover the pan and wait *1 minute*. The shrimp should then be just opaque and tender. Do not overcook. Lift the shrimp from the water with a slotted spoon and drain them. Combine shrimp and cashews in the top of a double boiler and keep them warm over warm, not boiling, water while the sauce is made.

Measure ¼ cup of the cooking liquid and combine it with the cornstarch and ginger. Bring to a boil and simmer, stirring, until it is thickened. This will take only a minute or so. Very gently stir just enough sauce into the shrimp and cashews to moisten them and give them a glossy coating. Serve at once. Do not add salt; this dish is bland on purpose. You will very much appreciate it as a break from spicy dishes.

* If frozen shrimp only are available, use them. Do not cover; watch very carefully. Remove from heat and rinse with cold water as soon as they are opaque.
† If only salted nuts are available, wash them.

SAUTÉED WHOLE FISH

This is a basic recipe—it may be thought of as a first step in preparing many Chinese dishes.

1 white-fleshed fish, about 4 pounds
½ cup flour, cornstarch, or rice starch
lard or oil·for frying

Wash and dry the fish; leave the head, tail, and fins on. Sift enough flour over the fish to coat it well, then shake to remove the excess flour.

Meanwhile, heat enough lard or oil in a skillet large enough to hold the fish to make the fat 1″ deep. If you have a frying thermometer, now is the time to use it: Heat the fat to 360° F. If you do not have a thermometer, heat the fat over a brisk fire until it is hot but not smoking. Put the fish in the skillet and cook about a minute on each side. Turn the heat down and cook another 5 or 6 minutes, turning once. The fish is ready to remove when a meat thermometer inserted in the thickest part of the flesh registers 145° F. If you do not have a thermometer, time the fish carefully and remove it when it is just browned nicely and before the fish "flakes," a sign that it is already overdone. It will continue to cook even after it is removed from the hot oil. A fish that is to be eaten plain, with soy sauce as seasoning and some sautéed vegetables on the side, needs a little more cooking than one to be reheated with sauce. Rescue the one to be reused as soon as it is a nice color.

SAUTÉED FISH WITH CLEAR GINGER SAUCE

1 **whole sautéed 4-pound fish (See Sautéed Whole Fish.)**
¼ **cup soy sauce**
¼ **cup sweet sherry**
1 **teaspoon salt**
1 **piece of fresh ginger about 3″ × ½″, sliced thin**
4 **scallions or 1 small onion, diced**
1 **cup water**
1 **tablespoon lard or oil**

There are two ways (that I know of) to go about this dish:

1. If you are sautéing and saucing the fish at one time and can, therefore, control very well the degree to which the fish cooks, you would not remove the fish from the skillet but instead pour off all but 1 tablespoon of the cooking oil. (1 tablespoon in the skillet and around the fish will be what remains when you drain the fish pretty thoroughly.) Add the rest of the ingredients to the skillet, increase the heat, and cook at a brisk simmer for about 10 minutes.

2. If you do the sautéing beforehand (restaurants sometimes do this), start by combining all the ingredients except the fish in a pan big enough to hold the fish and sauce. Increase the water to 1¼ cup. Cook briskly for 10 minutes, then add the sautéed fish. Heat only enough to warm up the fish, about 5 minutes, at a very low simmer, covered.

Both methods yield a delicious and different fish dish. It can be served hot or cold, and some cooks even say their sauce jells when it is cold; so far that hasn't happened for me, but maybe you will have better luck and a more cooperative fish.

Sautéed Whole Fish (page 88) served with brown sauce and vegetables

POACHED FISH WITH VEGETABLES

- **2 fillets, about ½ pound, firm white-fleshed fish**
  unsalted chicken broth or water to cover fish
- **3 tablespoons dry rice wine or other dry white wine**
- **½ cup dark green vegetable, such as snow peas or broccoli**
- **¼ cup light green or yellow or white vegetables, such as bamboo shoots, celery, or water chestnuts**
- **1 teaspoon oil**
- **2 teaspoons cornstarch**
- **½ teaspoon salt**
- **½ teaspoon white pepper**

Wipe the fish with a damp cloth or paper towels; do not wash. In a separate saucepan, bring about 2 cups of chicken broth to a boil. In the saucepan in which the fish is to be poached, place the fillets and the wine. Add enough boiling broth just to cover the fillets and cook over very low heat until the fish is done, about 7 minutes. Check the fish often and do not overcook—it will be done when it is barely opaque. Treat it gently because it will be very, very tender.

Remove the fish from the poaching liquid and drain on a rack; keep warm. Wash and dry the raw vegetables and separate them into small uniform flowerets, slices, or whatever. (Leave snow peas whole, of course.) Thoroughly dry canned vegetables. Heat the oil in a skillet and add the raw vegetables; cook 1 minute, tossing to coat with oil. Cover and cook 2 minutes. Add the canned vegetables, if any, and ½ cup of the poaching liquid mixed with the cornstarch, salt, and pepper. Cook, stirring constantly, until the sauce is thickened. This should take only a few moments.

Carefully transfer the poached fish back to the skillet and heat just enough to make sure it is coated with sauce and hot through. Break into bite-sized pieces (not too small) and gently transfer the dish to a warm serving platter. Serve at once.

N.B. This dish is very delicate and must be eaten when it is ready to be enjoyed at its best. It takes very little time if all the ingredients are prepared and measured beforehand; don't start cooking it until your diners are ready to start eating.

PORK

PORK

Pork is a great staple in Chinese cooking and eating. When "meat" is mentioned, unless some other notice is given, it is pork.

Besides being authentic, pork is almost always available here, it is usually cheaper than beef, and it is very good nutritionally. The B vitamins it contains would be destroyed by overcooking, an offense most Chinese recipes do not commit against their ingredients.

In most of the recipes in this section, beef could be substituted for pork. The beef would need to cook a little longer, and it would need more oil, usually, to remain moist. The flavor of the dishes would be different, of course.

Chinese cooking uses every part of the pig—except, as the joke goes, the squeal. Pork-variety meats such as hogsheads, feet, tripe, liver, kidneys, and brains are often hard to get in supermarkets, but if you can find a specialty store that stocks them, do plan to try the recipes for them in this section. They are delicious and economical and superb nutritional bonuses.

The pork in the stir-fry and shredded dishes can come from pork chops, loins, or shoulders. Fresh ham would taste good, but it seems an extravagant choice when so many other cuts are available.

It is true that pork needs to be thoroughly cooked to avoid the danger of trichinosis, but by the time the pink color has left pork, it will have reached a high enough temperature to be entirely safe. Sliced and shredded pork cook very fast; in larger cuts, a meat thermometer is helpful. When it registers 150° F., the meat is done and perfectly safe but not overcooked.

BASIC BOILED PORK, WHOLE

1 whole fresh shoulder or ham, about 6 pounds, skin on and bone in
2 cups water
3 tablespoons sweet sherry
1 tablespoon sugar
1 tablespoon honey
1 cup soy sauce
1 piece fresh ginger about 1″ × ½″, sliced

Wash and dry the shoulder or ham. Place it, fat side down, in a heavy pot with a tight-fitting lid. Place over medium heat and cook until a little of the fat has rendered out. While the lean side is up, puncture it in several places with a skewer or a thin sharp knife. Turn the meat fat side up and add the water. Bring to a boil, add the other ingredients, cover and reduce the heat so that the liquid simmers. Cook very slowly until the meat is tender, about 2 hours. Test for doneness often if the meat is not tender at the end of 2 hours; you don't want to overcook it. Serve hot or cold.

BASIC BOILED PORK, CUT UP

To cook pieces of pork, cut them into 1½″ cubes; for 3 or 4 pounds of pork, reduce the water to 1 cup, the soy sauce to ½ cup, and eliminate the honey. Cook the same way as for whole shoulder or ham until the meat is tender, about 1 hour.

BOILED PORK WITH ROOT VEGETABLES

4 pounds pork cut in 1½″ cubes
2 pounds turnips, carrots, sweet radishes, or other root vegetable

Cook the pork as for Basic Boiled Pork, using 2 cups water and adding the sugar and the pared and cut-up vegetables for the last hour of cooking.

BOILED PORK WITH TIGER LILIES

Soak ¼ pound dried lily flowers in hot water for about an hour. Drain them and rinse well with cold water. Cook pork as for Boiled Pork with Root Vegetables, except add ½ teaspoon more sugar with lilies for the last ½ hour of cooking.

BOILED PORK WITH BAMBOO SHOOTS

Drain 1 can whole bamboo shoots. Cook pork as for Boiled Pork with Root Vegetables, except add ½ teaspoon more sugar with bamboo shoots, cut into chunks, for the last 10 minutes of cooking.

Ingredients for Basic Stir-Fry Pork Slices

BASIC STIR-FRY PORK SLICES

  ½ **pound lean boneless pork (Loin, shoulder, or chops would be good.)**
   1 **tablespoon soy sauce**
   2 **teaspoons sweet sherry**
1 ½ **teaspoons cornstarch**
   1 **tablespoon water**
   1 **tablespoon lard**

Cut the pork into very thin slices across the grain, then cut each slice into 2″ × 1″ pieces. Mix with the soy sauce, sherry, cornstarch, and water and toss to coat well.

Heat the lard in a heavy skillet.

So far this is basic sliced pork alone. There are many variations; all are delicious. From now on the cooking depends on the qualities of the vegetables used. If they cook fast, the pork is stir fried, then the vegetables added; if they cook slower than the meat, appropriate adjustments are made. The following variations are only a few of those possible but will show the timing necessary for various vegetable types.

BASIC STIR-FRY SHREDDED PORK

  ½ **pound lean boneless pork (chops, loin, or shoulder)**
  2 **teaspoons soy sauce**
  2 **teaspoons sweet sherry**
  1 **tablespoon lard**

Wipe the pork with a damp cloth or paper towels; dry thoroughly. Slice very thin, as for pork slices, then cut each slice again to make very thin shreds almost like matchsticks. Toss the pork shreds with the soy sauce and sherry. Heat the lard in a heavy skillet.

Pork shreds are not usually served alone; any vegetable may be combined and cooked with the meat. Combinations of two or more vegetables are also delicious. The basic recipe given above applies to all the following variations. Please note carefully the times and order of cooking for different vegetables.

TWICE-COOKED PORK

2 to 3 pounds pork loin, bone in
  water to cover

Wipe the pork with a damp cloth. Place in a deep pot with a tight lid and barely cover with water. Bring to a boil, cover and reduce heat so the broth simmers. Cook for 1 hour to 1½ hours, depending on size. Let the meat cool in the broth.

Remove the bones from the loin and slice it into pieces about 2″ × 1″. To cook again, you will need:

1 ½ tablespoons lard
  2 cloves garlic, sliced thin
  1 scallion, diced
  2 tablespoons soy sauce
  1 piece of fresh ginger ½″ × ½″, sliced

Heat the lard until very hot in a skillet. Add the garlic and mash to bring out flavor. Put in the sliced pork and cook, stirring constantly, for 2 or 3 minutes. Add the rest of the ingredients and cook 2 more minutes. Serve at once.

SLICED PORK WITH ROOT VEGETABLES

Prepare the sliced pork for cooking as in Basic Stir-Fry Pork Slices. Scrub and dry completely carrots or turnips or other root vegetable. Cut enough into matchstick pieces to make ⅔ cup. Put the vegetables into the hot fat and stir to coat them. Add 1 teaspoon water and cover the pan tightly for 2 minutes. Test the vegetables for tenderness; they should be barely tender but still crisp. If they are not done enough, cook, covered, another 30 seconds, then check again.

When the vegetables are crisp-tender, add 2 teaspoons lard to the skillet and let it heat. Add the pork, ½ teaspoon salt, and 1 teaspoon soy sauce and stir fry until it has lost its color and is tender, about 2 or 3 minutes. Serve at once.

SLICED PORK WITH MUSHROOMS

Soak 10 dried black mushrooms in hot water for 10 minutes. Drain them very well and dry with paper towels. Slice into thin pieces. Prepare the sliced pork for cooking as in Basic Stir-Fry Pork Slices. Put the pork into the hot fat and cook, stirring constantly, for 2 minutes. Add the mushrooms, 1 teaspoon soy sauce, and ½ teaspoon salt. Cook and stir another minute and serve.

SLICED PORK WITH RED AND GREEN PEPPERS

Slice ½ a red bell pepper and ½ a green bell pepper into ⅛″ slivers. (Discard seeds.) Cook with 1 tablespoon lard for 1 minute, then add sliced pork, 1 teaspoon soy sauce, and ½ teaspoon salt. Cook, stirring constantly, for 2 or 3 minutes. Serve at once.

SLICED PORK WITH BAMBOO SHOOTS

Prepare the sliced pork for cooking as in Basic Stir-Fry Pork Slices. Drain 1 can of sliced bamboo shoots well. Put the pork into the hot lard and sauté, stirring constantly, for 2 minutes. Then add the bamboo shoots, 1 teaspoon soy sauce, and ½ teaspoon salt. Cook and stir another minute and serve at once.

PORK SHREDS WITH BROCCOLI

Wash and dry broccoli and separate into very small (about ½")
flowerets. Slice some of the stalk, peeled, very thin and then shred
into pieces about the same size as the pork. You should have about
1 cup in all. Put the broccoli into the skillet when it is hot and
toss to coat the vegetable with oil. Stir fry 2 minutes; add seasoned
pork, 1 teaspoon soy sauce, and ½ teaspoon salt and cook another
2 minutes, stirring constantly. Serve at once.

PORK WITH SCALLIONS

Use 1 cup scallions, green and white parts, cut in ⅛" shreds. Start
the pork cooking and stir fry for 2 minutes. Add the scallion shreds
and stir for only 30 seconds more; they should be barely heated
through and still very crisp. Don't let them burn or brown at all.

The combinations for shredded pork and vegetables are endless.
The most important considerations are which vegetables are in beautiful condition and how the one chosen will cook with respect to
the pork. Bean or pea sprouts, for instance, can be added after
the pork has cooked 2 minutes; they require only 1 more minute
to be completely cooked. Asparagus works best if cut in ½" diagonal
slices and blanched in boiling water first; then add it after 2 minutes
and allow 2 more minutes cooking time. Add more lard or oil, very
sparingly, if the skillet is really dry at any point. Season with a
little more soy sauce and salt to your taste.

One shredded pork dish is such a staple in the Szechuan cuisine,
however, that the recipe for it is presented in full (page 119).

PORK SHREDS WITH BOK CHOY

Wash and dry the stalks of bok choy. Slice the dark green tops in shreds ¼"; peel the white base and cut into matchsticks about the size of the pork. If you have it, the heart of the bok choy head is a delicious addition; cut it even finer than the white part of the stems. You should have about 1½ cups in all.

Put the stems or heart of bok choy shreds into the skillet with the hot oil and stir fry for 1 minute. Add the pork and the dark green tops, 1 teaspoon soy sauce, ½ teaspoon salt, and ¼ teaspoon dry mustard to the skillet and cook 2 more minutes, stirring constantly.

MEATBALLS AND BOK CHOY

2 cups shredded (1" strips) bok choy
3 tablespoons water
2 teaspoons soy sauce
½ teaspoon salt
1 recipe Basic Minced Pork meatballs, about 6 (page 107)

Place the bok choy, water, soy sauce, and salt in a heavy pan with a tight-fitting lid. Arrange the meatballs on top of the vegetable. Bring the pot to a boil, quickly cover, and reduce heat so that the pot simmers. Check the bok choy for tenderness in 8 minutes; steam another minute or two if it is not tender.

Meatballs that are to be used in these dishes can be cooked a shorter time than the ones to be eaten plain, but it is not all that important. If the pork used has enough fat, the meatballs will be tender and juicy.

MEATBALLS AND CABBAGE

2 cups white cabbage shredded in ¼″ strips (Slice the heart very thin if
  it is used.)
¼ cup water
1 teaspoon lard
1 tablespoon soy sauce
¼ teaspoon sugar
1 recipe Basic Minced Pork meatballs **(page 107)**

Place the cabbage in a heavy pan with a tight lid. Add the rest
of the ingredients except the meatballs and bring to a boil. Place
the meatballs on top of the cabbage and cover the pot tightly. Reduce
the heat so that the cabbage just simmers. Check the cabbage in
10 minutes; it should be just crisp-tender.

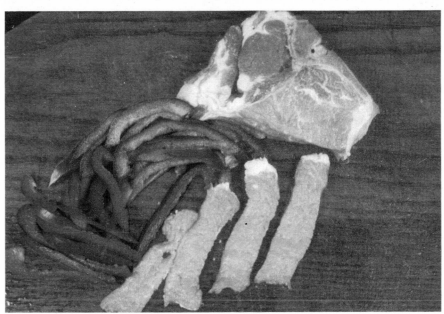

Ingredients for Sliced Pork with Red and Green Peppers (page 101)

PORK SHREDS WITH HOT AND SWEET PEPPERS

Seed and shred ½ a red bell pepper and ½ a green bell pepper very finely. Seed 1 hot green pepper (such as a chili serrano or a hot Italian green pepper) and mince it very finely. Stir fry the bell peppers for 30 seconds, then add pork shreds and 1 teaspoon soy sauce, ½ teaspoon salt, and 1 small clove of garlic, minced finely. Cook for 1 minute and 30 seconds, stirring all the time, then add the hot pepper and cook 30 seconds more. (If the hot pepper browns, it will turn very nasty!) Serve at once.

BASIC MINCED (GROUND) PORK

1 pound boneless pork with some fat on it, such as fatty pork chops or shoulder
1 tablespoon soy sauce
1 teaspoon sweet sherry
1 teaspoon sugar
2 tablespoon cornstarch
¼ teaspoon salt
½ teaspoon white pepper

Wipe the pork with a damp cloth; remove all tough fibers and ligaments. Mince finely. The traditional method uses heavy cleavers, but with patience and a sharp knife you can mince this much pork by hand. Begin by slicing it very thin, then shredding the slices, then chopping the shreds. The pork should not be gooey, but should retain the look of small *pieces* of meat. The mixture should be quite light pink; if it is not, add some more fat. It is also possible to grind the pork, though it won't have quite the same character and may tend to shrink more in cooking; but it is undeniably easier. Chill both the meat and the meat grinder thoroughly. (If the butcher grinds the pork for you, he should have the machine in the cold room; if he doesn't, find another butcher.) Cut the pork into cubes that will fit the grinder intake easily and grind quickly, using a coarse or medium blade. Put the ground meat back in the refrigerator at once and dismantle the grinder and *wash it thoroughly* in very hot water and soap. We don't want to be paranoid about trichinosis, but all the careful cooking of pork in the world won't help if equipment is contaminated.

Mix the minced pork with the rest of the ingredients and stir to combine thoroughly. Form the sausage into meatballs or small patties, depending on how they are to be used. Heat enough lard in a heavy skillet to give ¼" hot fat. Fry over medium heat, turning to brown on all sides, about 5 minutes in all (less time for tiny meatballs).

Meatballs can be served either hot or cold as a meat accompaniment for vegetable dishes. In that case, serve a mixture of half salt, half freshly ground black pepper for each diner to dip into. Tiny meatballs are excellent hors d'oeuvres.

Lions' Heads

LIONS' HEADS

This recipe is not from Szechuan, but it is very popular there. The city of Yangchow contributes this very good dish.

1 recipe Basic Minced Pork with the meat cut in slightly larger pieces or ground on a very coarse blade
broth (chicken or pork or whatever you have) seasoned with a little soy sauce, depending on how salty the broth is, for poaching
½ head bok choy

Mix the Minced Pork and form into 4 large balls; they should be about the size of good-sized peaches. Meanwhile, heat the broth in a large pot (wide, not necessarily deep) until it is just boiling. Reduce the heat so that it does not even shimmer and very carefully lower the meatballs into the liquid. Use a slotted spoon and a lot of patience. Cover the pot and let it stand 5 minutes. With luck this wait will keep the meatballs from disintegrating! Turn the heat up, watching carefully, and let the liquid just simmer. Cook covered for 15 minutes without disturbing, then check. The meatballs (Lions' Heads) should be almost done. When they are done (a meat thermometer removes the guesswork—145° F. is done), take them out of the broth and cook it hard to reduce it to ½ cup. Shred the bok choy into 1″ strips and place in the broth. Very carefully arrange the Lions' Heads on the bok choy. Bring the liquid to a boil, then reduce heat so it just simmers. Cover the pot and cook for about 10 minutes, or until the bok choy is tender-crisp. Serve hot or cold with a little soy sauce and rice vinegar mixed together.

Lions' heads may be sautéed, also, though it takes a great deal of patience, more fat, and very careful control of the heat to brown them and cook them inside simultaneously. Use enough oil to make 1″ in the skillet and keep the heat moderate to low. Let the lions' heads cook until brown on all sides, turning only when one spot is brown. This will probably take 20 to 30 minutes of constant watching. The crust is nice, but poaching is surely easier!

By the way, this is an extremely simplified version of this recipe. For the gung ho original, see Yangchow Lion's Head in *The Joy of Chinese Cooking* by Doreen Yen Hung Feng, Grosset & Dunlap, New York.

Mushrooms Stuffed with Minced Pork

MUSHROOMS STUFFED WITH MINCED PORK

Another use for Basic Minced Pork in its raw state is for stuffing mushroom caps—or tiny artichoke hearts, cabbage leaves, or whatever strikes your fancy. The finger-sized versions make spectacular hors d'oeuvres.

12 or 16 whole attractive dried black mushrooms or fresh mushrooms
1 tablespoon soy sauce
1 recipe Basic Minced Pork, raw
½ teaspoon white pepper

Soak the dry mushrooms in hot water for 10 minutes. Save the soaking liquid. Dry the reconstituted mushrooms and carefully remove the stems, leaving as attractive caps as possible. If fresh mushrooms are used, wipe them with a damp cloth and remove the stems. Brush the tops of the mushrooms with a little soy sauce.

On a rack that will fit into a steaming pot, arrange the mushrooms bottoms up. Stuff each one with enough of the minced pork mixture to make a pleasant mound. Brush the tops of the stuffed mushrooms (the meat) with the remaining soy sauce and sprinkle with pepper.

Add the mushroom-soaking water to the steaming pot and add enough hot water or chicken broth to cover the bottom of the pot 1″. Place the rack of stuffed mushrooms in the steamer and bring the liquid to a boil; cover the pot and reduce heat so that the liquid simmers and steams. Check the mushrooms in 5 minutes; if they are not tender enough, cook a little longer.

Stuffed mushrooms can also be cooked in a 350° F. oven. Arrange the mushrooms in a shallow pan that has been brushed with oil. Add a few tablespoons of water or unsalted chicken stock and bake 10 minutes. Watch carefully so that the pan does not dry and the mushrooms burn.

If the mushrooms are to be served as a main course, make a sauce from the steaming liquid or the liquid in the baking pan:

1 cup liquid from steaming or baking, or water
2 teaspoons cornstarch
1 teaspoon sweet sherry
1 tablespoon soy sauce
1 teaspoon peanut oil
  mushroom stems, sliced

Combine all ingredients and cook over medium heat until thickened. Pour over the stuffed mushrooms on the serving platter or pass separately.

If the mushrooms are to be served as an hors d'oeuvre, pass hot mustard.

ONIONS STUFFED WITH MINCED PORK

Another excellent variation of this dish is stuffed onions. Use large mild onions. Bake them in a 350° F. oven or parboil them in salted water just to cover until the centers will come out easily, leaving a shell about ¼″ thick. Stuff with the meat mixture and proceed as for stuffed mushrooms. For onions to serve as hors d'oeuvres, split 10 small (1″) mild onions and top with a mound of minced pork. Cook as for stuffed muchrooms.

BASIC RIBS WITH CABBAGE

1 recipe Basic Spareribs
1 cup shredded (¼″ pieces) white cabbage
1 tablespoon cider vinegar

Cook the spareribs according to the recipe for Basic Spareribs. When there is ½ hour of cooking time left to go, remove the ribs from the oven and drain the fat from the roasting pan under them. Return 3 tablespoons of the fat to the pan. Put the shredded cabbage in the pan and stir to coat well with the fat. Sprinkle vinegar over the cabbage, replace the rack with the ribs, and finish cooking. Stir the cabbage 2 or 3 times.

The proportions given in this recipe assume you are going to be serving several people and using several cups of cabbage. Reduce the fat and vinegar if less than 4 cups of cabbage are to be cooked. Also add a tablespoon of water to smaller batches of cabbage.

Pass soy sauce at the table.

Variation: Use ½ cup per person of sauerkraut (rinsed) or salted cabbage. (Canned from the Chinese grocery or homemade—see recipe in vegetable section.) Drain the preserved cabbage well and add when 15 minutes are left to cook the ribs. Stir to coat with fat and twice more to ensure even heating. Omit vinegar.

BOILED AND FRIED SPARERIBS

People who like Mexican food will recognize this as an old friend with a slight twist: carnitas with bones!

2 pounds spareribs
water barely to cover
3 tablespoons soy sauce
1 tablespoon salt
1 teaspoon sugar
1 tablespoon honey

Have the butcher cut the ribs into 1″ pieces across the bones. (You can separate the ribs at home.) Put the ribs mixed with the other ingredients in a very large skillet or heavy pan and add water just to cover. Bring to a boil, then turn down the heat so the meat cooks gently. It should not crowd the pan.

Cook until the liquid has boiled away. You will know when it has gone by the sizzling sound that comes from the pan. From now on you must watch the meat like a hawk. Stir and turn the pieces of ribs constantly; keep heat moderate and do not let them burn. When they are crisp, they are done. Serve at once. These riblets are very good with flour pancakes. No extra sauce is needed; it is cooked on them.

N.B. While very lean ribs are the ideal for most recipes, some fat is needed for this dish. It is unlikely that you will be offered ribs so lean that they would sabotage the cooking, but if so, stand up for fattier ribs!

BASIC SPARERIBS

1 pound spareribs for each person to be served

Heat the oven to 300° F. Wipe the ribs with a damp cloth and dry thoroughly. Cut into sections of 4 or 5 ribs, if you like, though the whole large piece (or more likely 2 pieces) will look more impressive.

Place the ribs on a rack over a roasting pan. (It should be fairly deep since a lot of fat will cook out of the ribs.) Place the ribs in the oven and cook until very done and tender, about 1½ hours. They will be crusty and dark brown, and best of all, you haven't had to do a thing to them!

The ribs can also be roasted longer at 250° F., say about 3½ hours. This is a good dish to make when you have to be away from home in the afternoon but must serve a memorable meal soon after getting back.

When the ribs are done, they are ready to receive any sauce you care to serve with them. Some good and traditional accompaniments include:

hot Chinese mustard
duk sauce (Buy it in the supermarket, near the water chestnuts.)
plain soy sauce
equal parts soy sauce and sherry simmered with a few slices of fresh ginger and 2 tablespoons chopped scallions

A nontraditional and very tasty sauce for ribs can be made from 1 cup whole-berry cranberry sauce and enough hot mustard to make it taste the way you want it to. For some reason this mixture is much better than the ingredients make it sound. A tablespoon or two of chopped scallions or onion would be good in this sauce, but not necessary; it is quite lively on its own!

BASIC PIG'S FEET

1 whole pig's foot for each person to be served (Cook some extra—the soup is wonderful.)
water barely to cover feet
½ cup soy sauce
1 teaspoon salt
¼ cup sweet sherry
1 piece fresh ginger 1″ × ½″, sliced

Wash the feet thoroughly; split them in half lengthwise with a cleaver or a heavy knife and a mallet. Heat a large heavy pot with a tight lid; place the dried feet in it and cook over moderate heat until browned on all sides. Do not crowd; do the browning in several batches if necessary.

When all the pieces are browned, return them to the pot and add the rest of the ingredients. Cover and reduce heat so the liquid barely simmers. Test after 2 hours; the feet should be very tender. Simmer longer, tightly covered, if necessary.

To serve, place a whole foot (2 halves) on each diner's plate. Strain the cooking liquid and serve separately as sauce. Also provide grated horseradish, hot mustard, fresh ground black pepper, and soy sauce for dipping.

Bok choy or white or red cabbage, sauerkraut, or salted cabbage are particularly good with pig's feet. Shred the raw vegetable and toss in a little oil in a skillet. Add a tablespoon of broth or water, cover tightly, and cook until crisp-tender, about 8 minutes. Rinse and drain sauerkraut or salted cabbage. Heat in fat just to warm through.

PIG'S FEET STUFFED WITH MEAT AND SPICES

1 **whole pig's foot for each person to be served**
1 **thin slice ham for each foot**
1 **scallion for each foot**
1 **water chestnut for each foot**
1 **teaspoon soy sauce per foot**
1 **slice bacon (smoked is all right here) per foot**
3 **Szechuan peppercorns, crushed, per foot**
  salt
  freshly ground black pepper
  sherry

Wash and dry the pig's feet and place in a heavy kettle. Barely cover with water and bring to a boil. Cover the pot and reduce heat to simmering. Cook about 30 minutes, or until the large bones in the feet move easily.

Drain the feet (save the broth—it is a beautiful beginning for all kinds of soup) and slit them up the back when they are cool enough to handle. Remove the large bones while disturbing the flesh as little as possible. Also try not to tear the skin.

While the feet boil, chop the ham, scallions, and water chestnuts into ¼″ pieces and stir with the soy sauce. Cook the bacon, cut into 1″ pieces, gently but do not brown. While the feet cool, combine all the rest of the ingredients with the ham mixture and the bacon, using enough sherry to make a moist stuffing mixture.

Spread the stuffing mixture inside the partially boned feet. Fold the feet back into shape and tie snugly with string. Over medium heat, heat the pan in which the bacon cooked; do not drain.

Place the stuffed feet in the pan and brown, keeping the heat moderate. Turn to brown on all sides. This will take some time since the heat must be kept low to prevent burning. When the feet are brown, test with a fork for tenderness. They should be very tender. If more cooking is needed, add a tablespoon or two of the broth or a tablespoon of sherry and a tablespoon of water, cover the pan tightly, and simmer over very low heat until feet are tender.

To serve, place the stuffed pig's feet on a warm platter and surround with a green vegetable cooked in some of the poaching broth. Pass the soy sauce separately.

Moo Shu Pork

MOO SHU PORK

¾ pound lean boneless pork
1 tablespoon soy sauce
2 tablespoons sweet sherry
½ teaspoon cornstarch
10 dried black mushrooms
¼ cup dried tiger lily blossoms
1 cup finely shredded firm vegetable (optional)*
3 tablespoons lard
1 teaspoon salt

Shred the pork into very thin matchsticks. Mix the soy sauce, sherry, and cornstarch and pour over the pork. Toss to coat the meat well. Let stand in the refrigerator until ready to cook.

Soak the mushrooms in hot water for at least 10 minutes, then drain and dry very thoroughly. Soak the tiger lilies in hot water for 1 hour, then rinse well in cold water and dry well with paper towels. If you are using another vegetable—bok choy, bamboo shoots, tiny broccoli flowerets, or celery—cut it finely. Slice the dry mushrooms into thin pieces.

Heat the lard in a heavy skillet but keep the heat moderate. Add the mushrooms and lily flowers to the skillet and toss to coat with fat. Cook gently for 3 minutes, then remove from pan and set aside. Stir fry the vegetable and pork, cooking the meat 2 minutes and the vegetable as much before adding it as is necessary for it to be crisp-tender. Add a little more lard to the skillet if it gets completely dry, but do it sparingly.

When the pork has cooked 2 minutes, return mushrooms and lilies to the pan and cook, stirring constantly, just long enough to heat through. Stir in salt and any of the soy sauce-sherry mixture that is left from marinating the pork. (If there is none left, use 2 teaspoons each of soy sauce and sherry and a pinch of cornstarch.) Stir around pan just enough to coat the meat and vegetables, then serve at once.

Flour pancakes (really *very* thin crepes) are served with Moo Shu Pork. See recipe in chapter on starches.

* Besides adding a nice texture to the dish, the vegetable makes it go farther, if that is a consideration. Choose a vegetable that will be somewhat crunchy when the dish is finished—and if nothing fresh seems to fill the bill, drained, canned bamboo shoots or water chestnuts are fine.

BEEF
&
LAMB

BEEF
&
LAMB

Beef is not used for food as much in China as it is in the United States, but there are some delicious recipes for it even so. Fillet (tenderloin) is the best cut to use for sliced and shredded dishes because it is tender and tasty. All the sliced and shredded beef dishes should cook very quickly—just until the meat loses its red color—so it is important that the meat be of the best quality.

Stews and hearty meat soups often use less elegant cuts of beef and are therefore both economical and tasty. Recipes for these dishes are in the chapter on soups.

Most of the recipes in the chapter on pork may be adapted for beef. Just keep in mind that the beef will have less fat in it and compensate with a little extra oil or lard. No extra cooking time is required. Experiment with your favorite pork combinations using beef; you will probably invent some new dishes!

SLICED BEEF IN JELLED BROTH

1 recipe Basic Boiled Beef made with a whole piece of meat
  watercress for garnish
  horseradish

This is an easy, elegant variation—or rather extension—of basic beef.

Let the meat cool in the broth. When it is cool enough to handle, remove it and set aside. Strain the cooking liquid and discard the onions and ginger. If you have cooked the meat very slowly, the broth should be quite clear, but if it is cloudy, clarify by lightly beating 1 egg white for each quart of broth and stirring it gently into the pot. Very slowly heat the broth just to simmering, turn off the heat, then strain the broth through two layers of cheesecloth.

Place the meat in a serving dish and add the clarified broth. Cover the dish and store in the refrigerator until the liquid jells, usually overnight. To serve, skim off any fat that has collected on top of the jelled broth. Unmold meat and broth onto a serving platter and garnish with watercress. Slice the meat thin and serve each portion with some of the jelled broth. Pass freshly grated horseradish at the table.

BASIC BOILED BEEF

  3 to 4 pounds shin or shank of beef cut in large chunks or the same
    amount of rump or bottom round in one chunk
1 ½ cups water
  ½ cup soy sauce
  2 tablespoons sweet sherry
  3 scallions or 1 small onion, sliced
  1 piece of fresh ginger about 1″ × ½″, sliced

Put the meat in a heavy pot with a tight lid. Add the water and bring it to a boil. Add the rest of the ingredients and bring to a boil again. Now cover and reduce the heat so the liquid barely simmers. Cook very slowly until the meat is very, very tender, probably 3 or 4 hours.

If you have used shin or shank, the liquid will jell when it cools, and any fat will be easy to remove. The meat is even better reheated in the juice than it was the first time!

BEEF WITH ONIONS

½ **pound fillet of beef**
2 **large mild onions (or 10 scallions, green part and all)**
1 **teaspoon sugar**
2 **teaspoons sweet sherry**
2 **teaspoons soy sauce**
1 **teaspoon salt**
1 **tablespoon oil**

Remove all fat and membrane from the beef and cut it into very thin pieces 1½″ × ½″. Slice the onions thin, then cut each slice in half. Mix the rest of the ingredients except the oil with the beef and toss well.

Heat the oil in a skillet. Add the onions and cook for about 3 minutes; they should not brown at all. Remove the onions and set aside. Add the steak slices to the pan and cook very quickly, stirring constantly. (If the skillet is very dry, add a little more oil to cook the beef.) Return the onions to the pan and stir only to heat through. Serve at once.

This recipe is also good made with shredded beef: Cut each slice so that very thin matchsticks of beef are made. Fillet is easier to slice thin if it is very cold or slightly frozen.

Ingredients for Kung Pao Steak

KUNG PAO STEAK

½ pound fillet of beef
10 dried black mushrooms
2 chilis serranos (or hot green Italian peppers)
½ cup sliced bamboo shoots
½ cup almonds
1 tablespoon oil
3 cloves garlic, sliced
1 tablespoon soy sauce
1 tablespoon sweet sherry
½ cup raw snow peas

Cut the steak into very thin slices after removing all the fat and membranes. Cut each slice into pieces about 1″ × ½″. Soak the mushrooms in hot water for 5 minutes, then drain and slice in thin slivers. Seed the chilis and slice them in very small slivers. Toast the almonds lightly in a moderate oven (or use toasted whole nuts).

Heat the oil in a heavy skillet. Add the beef and cook quickly, stirring constantly. This should take only a minute or two. Add the rest of the ingredients, including the snow peas, and stir well. Cover and cook for 2 minutes. The peas should be barely tender and still bright green. Serve at once.

Ingredients for Oxtail Stew

OXTAIL STEW

2 to 3 pounds oxtail cut in 1″ sections (This is how it is usually packaged at the supermarket.)
1 quart water
½ cup soy sauce
¼ cup dry sherry
1 piece of fresh ginger about 2″ × ½″, sliced
2 cups vegetable of choice or combination of vegetables
1 cup diced celery

Wipe the oxtail pieces with a damp cloth to remove any bone dust that might be clinging to them where they were cut up—it isn't so tasty in the stew. Place the oxtail in a large heavy kettle with a tight lid. Add the water and bring to a rolling boil. Add the soy sauce, sherry, and fresh ginger (if fresh ginger is not available, use ½ teaspoon fresh ground ginger—not as good but better than none) and bring liquid to a boil again. Cover the pot and simmer until the oxtail meat is very tender and falls off the bone. Let the stew cool a little, then remove the bones. This is easier if you have a large slotted spoon or a colander through which to strain the broth. Discard the bones or put them in another pot of soup; there won't be much taste left in them, but the texture they impart will be nice. Skim off all the fat you can, or better yet, put the broth and meat in the refrigerator overnight. Then the fat will be very easy to remove.

Reheat the stew; if you wish to add vegetables, cut them in attractive chunks and simmer in stew for the time required to cook them tender. Add the celery the last 15 minutes for greenery and crunchiness.

Leg of Mutton Chinese Style

Lamb and mutton are not very popular in China. Two dishes have developed, however, that are very good and deserve your attention. The first is Lamb Tripe with Coriander; see the recipe in the section on pork. The second is Leg of Mutton Chinese Style. That not very glamorous cut is something beautiful cooked this way.

LEG OF MUTTON CHINESE STYLE

1 butt end of a whole leg of mutton or lamb
6 cloves garlic, sliced
3 quarts water
3 cups soy sauce
1 cup sweet sherry
1 large onion, sliced

Wipe the meat with a damp cloth and place it in a pot with a lid large enough to hold it. Add the rest of the ingredients and bring to a boil. Turn the leg every 30 minutes if the broth does not cover it. Cook covered at a simmer until the leg is tender, about 2 or 3 hours depending on its size.

When the leg is tender, you may remove it from the broth and brown the fat side in a 550° F. oven for about 10 minutes, or you may eat it directly from the pot. Vegetables may be added to the pot, also. Either way, a garnish of parsley or watercress is nice.

THE
INSIDE
OF
THE
ANIMAL

THE INSIDE OF THE ANIMAL

For many centuries in China there have been many, many people who have had to be fed with a finite amount of food. There were very few (if any) frontiers offering virgin lands and amounts of edibles sufficient to waste. Therefore, the cuisine developed that most admirable of remedies, the elegant solution: Make delectable use of all food. In the West, and in the United States in particular, we have had such plenty that except for families that raise their food we have wasted (as a group) more than we have eaten. It is possible that we might go on for a time throwing out all the inside of the animal, but, ecological considerations aside, we have, most of us, been missing both delightful tastes and excellent nutrition.

Tripe is mostly discarded in this country; not long ago liver was known as cats' meat. (Wouldn't you rather look like a cat than an advertisement for Weight Watchers—before?) Kidneys are scorned, and not one person in a hundred has laid tooth to tongue, heart, brains, or sweetbreads. There is a sad and, it seems, almost genetic revulsion to eating the most vitally functioning parts of food animals.

If you like to cook, if you like to eat, and if you have had trouble approaching the insides of food animals in the kitchen, the recipes in the next pages may help. If you are a believer already, you may recognize old favorites; people who love to cook and eat seem to be simultaneous inventors first class!

TRIPE

The thing about tripe is that it was once, and not so long ago, the outside part of an intestine. Whether it is from the pervasive influence of toilet training on the generation now mostly wielding power in the kitchen or from some other, darker influence, the most common attitude toward tripe among otherwise good and sensitive cooks is, "Oh my God, NO!"

To be sure, careless slaughterhouses and butchers have a lot to answer for. When an animal is slaughtered, the man cutting the animal up has many chances to pierce the intestines and contaminate the outside portion with fecal matter. Such contamination need not be dangerous (boiling does wonderful things), but it is certainly not going to make a purchaser of the tripe in question dance and sing. And to be fair, it is often very difficult to extract the edible tripe in the best possible condition. But it can be done; indeed, it is done. Otherwise, half the Continental restaurants in metropolitan areas would have to shut down tomorrow. The question, then, boils down to getting good tripe and then knowing how to cook it. To get quality tripe, fix a custom butcher (there is nobody to blame at the supermarket if the worst happens) with a beady eye and tell him you want x pounds of y, z tripe. X: If you can freeze it, ask for 2 or 3 pounds; if you can't store it yourself, demand the quantity you really need. The larger amount is more impressive, but then you've *got* it. Y: This designates whether you want honeycomb, flat, or straight tripe. Honeycomb looks like it sounds: beeswax in the hive. Flat tripe comes in a sheet and is easier to work with. Straight tripe, usually sold only from lamb, looks like white empty sausage casings. Z is the animal from which you want the tripe. There is not much difference in the intrinsic qualities of different animals' tripe; mostly, the size of the animal determines the size of the tripe, and that's about it. In general, ask for flat tripe (of whatever animal) and see what happens. Remember to look stern. Then you can deal with the butcher and settle for whatever he can supply—if it is of good quality. Place your order several days before you need the tripe; the butcher may not usually carry it and may have to buy it at the wholesale market. This is some trouble for you but a very good sign; at least you aren't getting last week's tripe!

Before getting on to the cooking, we must deal with what is good-quality tripe. Whatever type and kind, it will be clean and white or whitish. It will smell something like a new shoe or a new book or a hot day in a tropical port, depending on your experiences and associations. What it will *not* smell like, if you want it, is intestinal waste. When you begin to cook it, there may be whiffs of odors you don't care for, but they shouldn't overcome you. Persevere through 2 or 3 changes of water. If there is no improvement, you can take the tripe back to the butcher and say that it doesn't meet your standards. Don't go into particulars; he can't argue with your flat statement. You may not get your money back (not much, since it is so cheap), but you will know to go to another store next time. But on the point of good tripe, to summarize: As it cooks the first two or three times, it will *not* smell very good. Don't worry. If it smells foul, take it back.

Hang in there.

Proper cooking starts with thorough precooking. See the recipe for Basic Pork Tripe. It works for other kinds as well. The meat should be fork-tender, and the broth should be smelling like something edible, if a little like LePage glue.

Cooked tripe can be used in all recipes for sliced pork or shredded pork; cut in the appropriate pieces and add to the cooking pan for just enough time to heat through. Slices of tripe may be sizzled in hot fat to brown on both sides before adding to other ingredients.

Tripe with Coriander

TRIPE WITH CORIANDER

This is mostly a Hunan dish using lamb or beef tripe, but pork tripe works fine and is often easier to find.

½ pound cooked (according to you) tripe—save the other half pound for another time; freeze it **(see Basic Pork Tripe, page 140)**
1 chili pasilla about 7″ long
1 tablespoon lard or peanut oil (lard is better)
¾ cup unsalted chicken stock or water
1 tablespoon soy sauce
1 clove garlic, chopped fine
½ teaspoon sugar
6 dried black mushrooms soaked for 10 minutes in hot water
½ cup chopped fresh coriander, stems and all
2 or 3 sprigs whole fresh coriander for garnish

Cut the tripe into fine slivers; it should look like matchsticks about 2½″ long. Dry well with paper towels.

Barely cover the chili with hot water and let it stand 10 minutes. Carefully cut it into ⅛″ slices. Remove the seeds and discard them—they are much too hot. Dry chili slices with paper towels.

In a heavy skillet heat the lard or oil until it is very hot. Toss the chili slices in the fat for a moment to coat; let them wilt, but do not let them burn. Reduce heat and add stock, soy sauce, garlic, and sugar; simmer about 10 minutes.

Drain the mushrooms and cut them in ⅛″ slices. Dry thoroughly. Add tripe shreds and mushrooms to sauce and stir to coat; cook just enough to heat through. Stir in chopped coriander and remove from heat at once. Transfer to a warm serving dish and garnish with sprigs of fresh coriander; serve at once. Flour pancakes are very good with this dish.

BASIC PORK TRIPE

1 pound cleaned tripe
  water
  salt
  lemon slices

Rinse the tripe well in cold water. Put it in a heavy pan and cover with water. Add 1 teaspoon salt and a ¼″ slice of lemon. Bring the water to a boil and cook about 5 minutes. Pour the water off, rinse the tripe, and start all over. Repeat this process until the tripe smells like meat (rather than something else!) cooking. Three or four changes of water are usually enough. When it smells acceptable (all this is assuming the tripe came from the butcher raw), cover the pot and simmer until the tripe is very tender; a fork should go through it easily. Drain and cool. It is now ready for most recipes. It usually takes a long morning or a whole day to get the tripe to this stage, so plan accordingly.

If you bought the tripe cooked, steamed, or whatever your part of the country calls it, bring it to a boil in some salted, lemoned water, anyway. Their definition of cooked may not be yours. If any deficiencies appear, proceed as above.

Usually tripe will be needed cut in squares or in small matchsticks. If it seems hard to cut, consider that it (1) needs more cooking or (2) would benefit from being frozen solid. Freezing makes fancy cutting much easier, and a thorough chilling never hurt anything.

BRAISED TRIPE WITH SOY AND GINGER SAUCE

 1 **pound tripe, precooked, (see Basic Pork Tripe) in one piece**
   water barely to cover
 2 **tablespoons soy sauce**
 2 **tablespoons sweet sherry**
½ **cup chopped scallions or onions**
 1 **piece fresh ginger about 1″ × ½″, sliced**
½ **teaspoon dry mustard**
 1 **teaspoon cornstarch**

Combine all ingredients except mustard and cornstarch in a heavy pot with a tight-fitting lid. Bring liquid to a boil, cover, then reduce heat so that pot simmers. Cook for 1 hour; test tripe—it should be very, very tender. Cook at higher heat for 15 minutes to reduce liquid. Remove tripe and add mustard and cornstarch, mixed with a little cold water. Cook and stir until thickened. Cut the tripe into thin strips and arrange on a serving plate. Pour the sauce over tripe and serve at once. Pass freshly ground pepper.

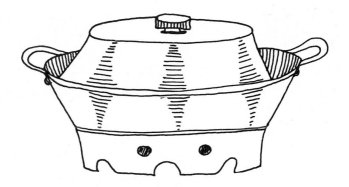

Tripe Simmered with Vegetables

TRIPE SIMMERED WITH VEGETABLES

2 pounds raw tripe, parboiled
4 cups water
¼ cup soy sauce
½ cup sherry
2 whole scallions, sliced
2 cups vegetables

When the tripe has been parboiled until it smells good, put it in a big pot with the water and cook it, barely simmering, until it is tender, about 2 hours. Remove the tripe and cut it into 1″ squares. Return to the pot and add the soy sauce, sherry, and scallions. Cook another hour. The tripe stew can be served as it is, or vegetables can be added during the final hour of cooking. Cut the vegetables into attractive chunks and add so that they are just tender when the stew is done. For instance, add carrots or turnips (or a combination of the two) at the beginning of the final hour. Sliced onions, peppers, shredded cabbage, broccoli, or cauliflower would go into the pot for the last 15 minutes.

KIDNEYS

Kidneys—pork, beef, lamb, or veal—can be delicious, and they are very good for you, but they can also be ruined by improper handling before and during cooking.

Before you wash the kidneys, cut away and discard *all* the white membranes and tubes. It is the white material that contains the unpleasant odor associated with kidneys, and if it gets wet, that odor will permeate the edible part of the organ as well. Fingernail scissors are a good tool to remove the membranes.

When all the membranes are gone, wash the kidneys quickly in cold water and dry thoroughly with paper towels; do not soak them. Slice or shred the meat and use in any recipe calling for meat slices or shreds. The kidney meat cooks in 3 minutes, so no adjustment is necessary in the timing of most recipes. Do not overcook and do serve at once; kidneys aren't good the second time around!

Recipes that are especially good with kidneys include:

Sliced Pork with Red and Green Peppers

Pork Shreds with Scallions

KIDNEY WITH PEPPERS AND ONIONS

1 cup kidney meat cut in thin slices about 1½″ × ½″
2 tablespoons soy sauce
1 tablespoon cornstarch
1 teaspoon salt
1 tablespoon sweet sherry
1 large green pepper cut in ¼″ slivers
1 large mild onion thinly sliced
2 tablespoons lard

Mix the kidney with the soy sauce, cornstarch, salt, and sherry. Slice the pepper and the onion. Heat half the lard in a heavy skillet and stir fry the pepper until it begins to wilt, about 3 minutes. Add the rest of the lard and the kidney and onion. Cook another 3 minutes, stirring constantly. Serve at once. Pass the soy sauce and freshly ground black pepper at the table.

SIMMERED AND FRIED BRAINS

1 set calf's or beef brains
¼ cup unsalted chicken broth or water
2 teaspoons soy sauce
2 teaspoons sweet sherry
1 tablespoon oil
1 scallion, chopped, for garnish

Cut the brains into 1½″ squares. Place in a heavy skillet with a lid and add the rest of the ingredients except the oil and scallions. Bring to a boil, then reduce heat and simmer covered for 10 minutes. Remove cover and turn the heat up to moderate. The brains should be set and firmer now. Watch the pan carefully. When the liquid is very low, add the oil. When the pan begins to sizzle, stir and fry the brains for 2 minutes. They should be lightly browned. Turn so that all sides of the pieces cook.

Put on a warmed serving plate and garnish with chopped scallions. Pass the soy sauce at the table.

LIVER

Pork liver is one of the least expensive and most delicious treats available today; it is romping with iron and other nutrients. Beef and lamb liver are also good buys—lamb has an excellent supply of vitamin A, while beef tops veal in vitamin A and has fewer calories per serving.

Liver of any kind should not be overcooked. To use it in recipes for chicken livers or for sliced meat, have liver cut thin (about ¼″) by the butcher. If you buy packaged liver that is thicker, freeze it to make slicing easier. Or place the thick slice between two plates, the bottom one top down, the upper one top up, and slice the liver while pressing firmly on the top plate. Cut the thin slices into 1″ × 1″ pieces. Cut 1″ × ½″ pieces for recipes requiring shredded meat. Whatever the recipe, cook the liver only until it loses its red color. It will be done from the heat already present by the time the dish is served.

Pork liver—or beef or lamb liver—are especially good in the following recipes. Just substitute liver for the meat component and adjust cooking time:

> Sliced Pork with Red and Green Peppers
> Pork with Scallions

LIVER WITH MUSHROOMS AND ONIONS

½ pound liver, sliced thin and cut in 1″ squares
1 tablespoon lard or oil
6 dried black mushrooms, soaked 10 minutes in hot water
6 whole scallions or 1 medium onion, chopped
2 tablespoons soy sauce
1 teaspoon sugar

Dry liver. Heat lard in a heavy skillet. Meanwhile, drain the mushrooms and dry them well; slice ⅛″ thick. Place liver in skillet and cook 1 minute; turn each piece. Add mushrooms and chopped scallions or onion. Stir to coat with fat and cook 1 minute. Pour in soy sauce and sprinkle on sugar; stir and heat so that meat and vegetables are coated. Serve at once. Pass lemon or lime slices to squeeze on the liver.

VEGETABLES

VEGETABLES

Vegetables alone are not served as often in China as they are here since they are usually incorporated in at least one of the other dishes being served. Whether they are to be ingredients in a complex recipe or served on their own, however, the first consideration is that the vegetables chosen be very fresh and in good condition.

Of all methods of cooking, the one least used in China for vegetables is boiling. We now know that from a nutritional point of view, boiling is the least desirable way of cooking vegetables, so in following the Chinese method, we are doing ourselves a good turn as well. Chinese-style vegetables are not overcooked, another nutritional plus.

Vegetables with quite a high moisture content can be cooked beautifully and fast by stir frying. First, the vegetable should be washed and dried thoroughly, then cut into small uniform pieces. This not only speeds cooking but makes all the pieces cook at the same rate. Heat enough oil to cover the skillet to a depth of ¼". When it is hot, add the vegetable pieces and stir constantly to completely coat with oil. Most vegetables will cook in 2 or 3 minutes. If the vegetable you are cooking is not as tender as you wish it to be, or if it is one of the drier root vegetables, reduce the heat and cover the skillet for 2 minutes. When the vegetable is tender, drain all the oil from it before serving.

A combination of stir frying and steaming works well for many vegetables. Stir fry for 3 minutes, then add 1 or 2 teaspoons unsalted broth or water to the pan. Cover, reduce the heat, and allow to steam for 2 or 3 minutes. Check for tenderness. Do not overcook and be sure to drain the vegetable well before serving.

ROASTED SWEET POTATOES

Sweet potatoes are usually eaten as a snack in China, and they make a very good one, too.

1 medium-sized sweet potato per person

Wash and dry the sweet potatoes. Prick them well with a fork or sharp knife and place in a 325° F. oven for 1 hour or until tender. Let cool enough to eat or eat cold.

Sweet potatoes may be roasted on a *very* slow grill as well. In that case wash, dry, and prick them and wrap in two thicknesses of heavy-duty aluminum foil. Cook far away from the heat until the potatoes feel soft through the foil.

Fresh Vegetable Pickles

MILD FRESH PICKLES

2 cups sliced firm cucumbers
½ cup cider vinegar
1 teaspoon salt
1 teaspoon soy sauce

Select young tender cucumbers instead of the kind with tough waxy skins. Slice the young ones; peel and slice the tough-skinned ones. Bring the rest of the ingredients to a boil and pour over the cucumbers. Let marinate in the refrigerator 2 or 3 days, tightly covered.

Onions, green beans, or other crisp vegetables could be used with the cucumbers. A hot green pepper added whole is good, but then the pickles can no longer be called mild!

SALTED MUSTARD GREENS

2 pounds bright green mustard
2 tablespoons salt

Wash and pick over the mustard carefully. Dry with paper towels, then spread in the air to dry completely. Cut into 1½″ shreds and rub in the salt thoroughly.

Sterilize 4-pint glass canning jars and have two-piece lids on hand. Pack the mustard tightly into the jars (you may not need all 4—the greens compact a lot) so that there are no air spaces left. Seal and store in a cool place (not the refrigerator) for at least two weeks. It will turn yellow when it is ready to eat. Pour off the excess brine before using, or you may wish to rinse it in cold water for a milder flavor.

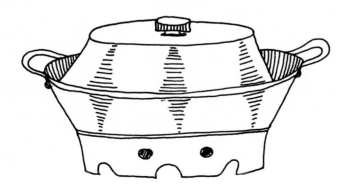

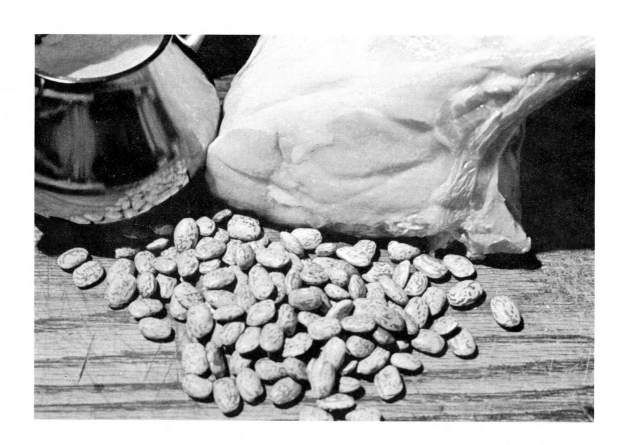

BEANS WITH PORK

1 pound dried beans—pinto, navy, or lima beans
2 pounds loin of pork, bone in
  salt
  sugar

Wash and look over the beans but do not soak them.

In a heavy pot with a tight lid brown the pork on all sides. Add the beans and enough water to cover them well. Add salt and sugar in the proportion of 1 teaspoon salt and ½ teaspoon sugar for each quart of water. Bring to a boil, then cover and reduce the heat so that the liquid barely simmers. Cook until the beans are tender, about 3 hours. Check the broth for seasonings; add more salt or soy sauce if necessary.

To serve, put pork on a serving dish and carve into thin slices. Put a slice of raw onion, then a slice of pork, in a soup bowl.

Add beans and broth.

This dish is even better cooked the day before it is to be eaten and reheated. It keeps well in the refrigerator, too.

Ingredients for Szechuan Marinated Vegetables

SZECHUAN MARINATED VEGETABLES
(Pickle Pot)

one very large earthenware pot or crock with a lid
firm vegetables in perfect condition; a suitable selection would include broccoli, cauliflower, green beans, bok choy, white cabbage, red cabbage, sweet radishes, turnips, green and yellow summer squash, red and green bell peppers, hot green peppers, cucumbers, and onions
a big pot of boiled, cool water
salt
garlic (optional, but why not?)
flour and water to make a stiff paste to seal the pot to the lid

Make sure the pot you plan to use is perfectly clean. Just for good measure, let it boil or wash it out thoroughly with boiling water and let drain dry.

Trim the vegetables and cut them into pieces or leave them whole. (The kind of vegetable dictates which: broccoli and cauliflower broken into flowerets, not too small; bell peppers halved and the seeds and stems discarded; hot green peppers left whole, green beans whole, onions whole, etc.) If you have to wash the vegetables (try not to), use the boiled water you have on hand.

Now arrange the vegetables in the pot. Put the sturdiest ones on the bottom. Add boiled water, keeping track of how much is used, to cover the vegetables by 2 or 3 inches. Add 1 tablespoon salt for each cup of water. Put the garlic in whole if you are using it. Seal up the pot with the flour paste and let stand for at least 2 weeks in a cool place. (You can add more vegetables as you use the ones in the pot.)

SOUPS

SOUPS

Soup is often served throughout the meal in China. A bland soup will cool down the spicy dishes; a perky one will pep up a mild meal. Almost every kind of soup imaginable is eaten, and the variations are endless, from clear unsalted chicken broth to thick stews.

The most important element in any soup, whatever kind it is, is the stock with which it starts. Begin the stock several days before you plan to use it so that it can cool and be defatted. It also seems to mellow, given a little time. Freeze stock not needed at once; it keeps very well.

BEEF SOUP WITH CARROTS OR TURNIPS

Use dark stock and beef in Pork and Cabbage Soup recipe. Add vegetables for the last hour of cooking. This is very close to our old friend, Mother's Vegetable Soup, and indeed can be made into it all the way by adding some green beans, diced celery, and diced onion for the last 15 minutes of the cooking time.

BROWN STOCK

4 or 5 pounds of beef bones, including a knuckle, if possible
1 pound stewing beef, shin preferably
   ingredients from recipe for White Stock
½ cup soy sauce

Wipe the beef bones to remove any bone dust left when they were sawed up. Heat a large heavy pot and brown the bones and meat well; careful browning over medium heat goes a long way to make both the color and taste of this stock right. Add the vegetables, soy sauce, and 4 or 5 quarts of water. Cook 4 or 5 hours, simmering gently, covered. Discard bones when stock is done; strain and discard vegetables (eat those you like) and defat the stock when it has become cold.

See the recipe for White Stock for method of defatting while the soup is still warm.

EGG DROP SOUP

4 cups chicken broth
½ teaspoons cornstarch
2 tablespoons water
2 eggs
   salt to taste

Heat the broth to boiling. Mix the cornstarch and water and add to the broth, stirring constantly while it thickens slightly. Beat the eggs very lightly and dribble into the hot but not boiling thickened stock. Taste for salt. Serve very hot.

There are dozens of variations on this soup. You might want to try adding 2 tablespoons minced cooked chicken breast to the soup. Some finely chopped watercress, about 1 tablespoon, would be good. Scallions are both pretty and tasty. A little minced ham is also nice.

WHITE STOCK

4 pounds chicken wings, necks, and backs (and some feet, if you can get them) or a stewing fowl
1 onion stuck with a whole clove
2 large carrots
3 or 4 stalks of celery, leaves and all
1 large parsnip
½ cup parsley

Wash the chicken parts or the chicken. If you use a whole bird, tie it up so it will hold its shape; you will have the advantage of cooked chicken meat for many recipes. Cut the vegetables roughly. Put everything in a large pot and add 5 quarts water (or water to cover, depending on the pot). Bring to a boil, then reduce the heat so that the liquid just simmers. Cook covered for 3 or 4 yours. Take out the chicken and strain stock. Let it get cold so fat will be easy to remove. Discard the vegetables used to make the stock (eat them yourself!), except possibly the carrots. If you save them, store in the refrigerator covered.

If you should have to defat the stock without waiting for it to get cold, pour it into a tall container, such as a milk bottle placed in the sink or a large pan; when the container is full, the fat will be at the top. Pour more stock in slowly so that the fat overflows and runs away. This is tedious and somewhat messy, but it is more effective than trying to skim a large container of stock.

PORK AND CABBAGE SOUP

8 cups white stock, or make stock from pork bones alone or in combination with chicken
2 pounds lean boneless pork
1 small head red or white cabbage or bok choy
soy sauce to taste

Heat the stock to boiling. In a skillet brown the meat, cut into 1½″ cubes, in a little lard. Put the pork in the stock and cook, barely simmering, until the pork is quite tender, about 1½ hours.

Shred the cabbage in ¼″ pieces and add to the soup. Continue to cook another 15 minutes or until the cabbage is quite tender but not disintegrating. Taste for seasoning and add soy sauce to taste.

PORK AND WATERCRESS SOUP

Follow directions for Pork and Cabbage Soup except add 1 cup chopped watercress leaves and 1 tablespoon cornstarch mixed with a little cold water to the stock for the last 15 minutes of cooking time. Sprinkle with grated fresh ginger (about ¼ teaspoon for each serving).

BEEF AND BOK CHOY SOUP

Use dark stock instead of white and beef instead of pork in the recipe for Pork and Cabbage Soup. Cook until the beef chunks are tender, about 2 hours. Add bok choy for last 8 minutes.

PORK AND BOK CHOY SOUP

Follow directions for Pork and Cabbage Soup except use 1 head bok choy cut in 1″ shreds and add it during the last 8 minutes of cooking time.

PORK SOUP WITH CARROTS OR TURNIPS

Follow directions for Pork and Cabbage Soup except use 2 cups carrots or turnips or a combination of the two cut into attractive chunks and add them for the last 45 minutes of cooking time.

BEEF SOUP WITH WATERCRESS

Use dark stock and beef in Pork and Cabbage Soup recipe. Add chopped watercress for the last 5 minutes of cooking time (no cornstarch in this version). Add ¼ cup dry sherry just before serving and taste for seasonings. Add soy sauce as needed. This is a very elegant soup indeed. You might want to cut the beef a little smaller (and neater) when making it.

STARCHES

STARCHES

Rice is basic to the cuisine in China, and since it is eaten with chopsticks there, a different texture in the cooked grain is needed. If you have prided yourself on your rice's separate, fluffy grains, you will need to learn a new method to make nice gluey rice. As we all know only too well, it isn't hard.

RICE

3 cups water
1 cup white rice

Bring the water to a boil and slowly stir in the rice. Cover the pan with a tight lid and reduce the heat as much as possible. Cook without stirring for about 40 minutes, or until all the water is absorbed. Do not add salt.

Rice cooked this way makes good rice pudding, too.

VERY QUICK SPRING ROLLS

The reason these are quick is that we use flour pancakes for the wrapping instead of starting a whole new batch of dough.

16 uncooked flour pancakes (page 173)
½ pound shredded pork or chopped shrimp or a combination of the two
1 scallion, finely chopped
½ cup fresh pea sprouts or canned bean sprouts
1 tablespoon soy sauce
1 generous tablespoon lard
  oil for frying

Mix all the ingredients except the lard and oil and toss to mix well. Heat the lard in a heavy pan and add the meat-vegetable mixture. Stir and cook for 3 minutes, then remove from the heat and let cool a little.

Lay a pancake flat and put a tablespoon of the filling just to one side of the diameter. Spread it slightly so it lies in a rectangle parallel to the diameter. Now fold in the ends of the pancake perpendicular to the filling, then fold the side of the circle nearest the filling over it and finish by rolling the folded part over the unused semicircle. If that flap shows signs of not sealing well, brush with a little beaten egg yolk.

This sounds more complicated than it really is. The main thing is to get the filling enclosed in the pastry somehow so it won't leak.

Heat enough oil to make ¼″ in the skillet. Fry the spring rolls until they are golden on each side. Do not crowd them.

To serve at once, slash each roll into 3 pieces diagonally and serve hot. Pass the soy sauce. If you are cooking ahead, drain the rolls, then reheat them in a 300° F. oven for 10 minutes before cutting and serving.

N.B. These are familiar appetizers, of course. Be sure to have plenty of napkins around if they are to be eaten with the fingers (perfectly proper, but greasy). Vary the filling according to your own ideas; almost any combination is good.

a

b

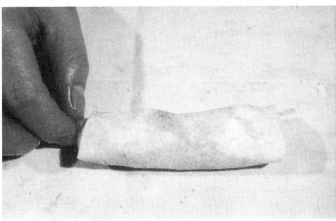

c

Very Quick Spring Rolls
*a) Place filling on dough. b) Fold back half of dough over
filling and fold ends toward each other. c) Roll forward
to seal front flap.*

Spring Rolls ready to serve (page 170)

FLOUR PANCAKES

These thin flour crepes are very good, especially with hot spicy meat dishes, and are classic with Moo Shu Pork. Many restaurants treat them like treasures and have to be persuaded to part with them; they seem to think two are enough for a serving, and they just are not.

2 cups flour
1 cup boiling water
   oil

Sift the flour and add the water which has just stopped boiling. Stir to make a dough and wrap it in foil or waxed paper when it cools slightly. Chill for an hour for easier handling.

When ready to cook, divide the dough into 16 balls. Place a piece of waxed paper on a smooth surface and brush it with oil. Pat a piece of dough into a flattened ball and place it on the paper. Brush the top of the dough with oil. Flatten another ball of dough and place it on top of the first one. Brush with oil and top with another sheet of waxed paper. Roll out to make 2 crepes about 5 or 6 inches in diameter. Repeat until all the dough is used up. To cook, heat a skillet or griddle over medium heat. Carefully separate the crepes and cook them one at a time for about 3 minutes on each side. They should not brown but only dry out somewhat. If they are to be eaten at once, place in a napkin-lined covered dish to keep hot. If you are cooking them ahead of time, wrap in foil and reheat on the griddle or in a slow oven when ready to eat.

DESSERTS

DESSERTS

Desserts as sweet conclusions to meals are not as popular in China as they are here. Sweet things are more likely to be eaten between meals as an energizing snack or with a light supper in the evening when the main meal has been in the middle of the day. Fruits in season are enjoyed, as are nuts and some vegetables. (See recipe for Roasted Sweet Potatoes.) Light sweet dishes are also sometimes served between courses of a large dinner; they break the pattern of fish and meat and vegetables.

FESTIVE RICE PUDDING

 2 **cups cooked rice**
 4 **eggs**
 2 **cups milk**
 ½ **cup candied fruits**
    sugar to taste—probably about ¼ cup
 1 **teaspoon vanilla flavoring**

Combine all ingredients in a mixing bowl and pour carefully into a greased baking dish. (A soufflé dish would be good.) Set dish in a larger pan of very hot water in a 325° F. oven and cook for about 30 minutes. Test for doneness with a knife blade about halfway from the edge of the pan to the center. When the blade is clean, the pudding is done. It should be a little liquid in the center.

Let the pudding stand a few minutes before serving. It will continue to cook a little bit and cool down enough to be eaten comfortably. If you can, make the pudding a few hours before it is to be eaten; it is at its very best when just at room temperature. Store any leftover pudding in the refrigerator and serve it cold. Reheating would spoil the custard, and letting it warm up would be asking for trouble from spoilage.

Festive Rice Pudding is a Westernized version of Chinese rice pudding, which has no milk or eggs. In fact, it is actually steamed sweetened rice with fruit and is called Eight-Jewel Rice Pudding.

EIGHT-JEWEL RICE PUDDING

1 pound short grain white rice
3 cups water
½ cup sugar
an assortment of pretty candied fruit, about ¼ pound

Put the rice and 2 cups of water in a *large* heavy pan and bring to a boil. Simmer until the rice grains look transparent around the edges but still opaque in the middle. Add the other cup of water and the sugar, bring to a boil, then reduce heat and cook 15 minutes more. This whole process will take about 45 minutes, more or less, depending on the rice.

In a large heatproof bowl* arrange the fruit in an attractive design. Half slices of pineapple make butterflies with citron antennae and cherry spots, for instance. Let the artist in you take over. Carefully spoon the rice mixture on top of the fruit, being careful not to displace your design. Put the bowl of pudding on a rack in a covered steaming pot and steam for about 3 hours. The rice should be very tender and the pudding firm. Remove it from the steamer and unmold (run a knife around the edge to loosen it before you try this!) onto a large serving platter. If there are leftovers, store covered in the refrigerator and steam again before serving. This dish is always served hot.

* It is very un-Chinese of me to suggest it, but I think that bowl ought to be well greased with solid vegetable shortening or butter.

CRACKLING BANANAS I

1 cup honey
½ cup sugar
½ cup water
1 teaspoon cider vinegar
1 or 2 bananas for each diner; the bananas should be barely ripe
   a large shallow bowl of water with ice cubes in it

Combine the honey, sugar, water, and vinegar in a saucepan and cook until it reaches 275° F. on a candy thermometer (soft-crack stage). If you do not have a thermometer, cook until a bit of the syrup dropped in cold water separates into firm threads. Meanwhile, cut the bananas into 1″ chunks and arrange them in a shallow bowl. Have chopsticks handy; they are really the best implements for dealing with this dish. Prepare the ice water.

When the syrup is ready, pour it over the banana chunks. Try to coat them thoroughly, but handle the fruit gently. Take to the table with haste and serve. Each diner takes a bit of banana with his chopsticks and dips it in the ice water. The cold hardens the syrup and voilà! Crackling Bananas.

CRACKLING PEARS

Make syrup as for Crackling Bananas I. Choose ripe but firm pears, 1 per person. Peel and core and cut in 8 chunks each. Sprinkle a little grated fresh ginger, about ½ teaspoon, over pears before pouring on the syrup.

CRACKLING APPLES

Make syrup as for Crackling Bananas I, but omit the vinegar. Choose firm-fleshed apples such as Delicious or Rome Beauty, one per person. Core and peel the apples and cut in bite-sized chunks. Sprinkle with lemon to keep the apples from turning dark while the syrup cooks. (That's why the vinegar is omitted from the syrup; there will be a touch of tartness in the apples already.)

Crackling Bananas

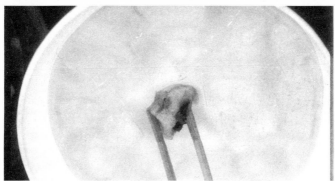

Sautéed bananas and ice water. Each person dips a piece of banana in the ice water with his chopstick. The low temperature of the water sets the syrup and makes the "crackle."

CRACKLING BANANAS II

1 **barely ripe banana for each diner**
1 **tablespoon oil**
2 **tablespoons sugar**

SYRUP
⅔ **cup sugar**
⅓ **cup cider vinegar**
1 **tablespoon cornstarch**
  dash soy sauce

Cut the bananas into chunks. Heat the oil in a skillet and add the bananas. Coat well with the oil and cook very, very slowly, turning often but gently. When they are glazed but still firm, sprinkle 2 tablespoons sugar over them. Turn once more, then remove to a serving plate.

To make the syrup, combine the sugar and vinegar and boil it vigorously for 3 minutes. Mix the cornstarch, soy sauce, and a little cold water together. Take the syrup off the heat, then add the cornstarch mixture, stirring constantly. Return to the heat and cook until the syrup is very stiff, only a minute or two. Pour the syrup over the bananas and coat each chunk well. Serve at once and let each diner dip pieces into a bowl of ice water with chopsticks to harden the syrup.

This method of cooking is faster than the first version, but aside from that it isn't that much of an improvement. Pears and apples can also be done this way, but don't try to sauté the pears; you will have instant pear jam on your hands.

BISCUITS WITH SESAME SEEDS AND HONEY

1 recipe of your favorite biscuit method
½ cup honey
¼ cup sesame seeds

Make the biscuits, roll them out thinner than usual, and cut out. (If you do not have a favorite biscuit method, may I recommend 2 cups Bisquick mixed with ¼ cup water; very good, and it couldn't be simpler.)

Put the honey in a small saucepan and start it heating over low heat. Heat the oven to 425° F. Place the biscuits on a *greased* baking sheet and start baking them when the oven is hot.

When the biscuits are firm but not browned, brush the tops with the warm honey and sprinkle scantily with sesame seeds. Repeat the process 3 times as the biscuits finish browning. When they are quite dark brown, remove from the baking sheet at once and let cool on a rack; some of the honey is bound to drip onto the baking sheet, and if the biscuits cool there, it will be impossible to get them off without tearing them up.

Sesame biscuits are good hot or cold, plain or fancy. They are almost sinfully good split, toasted with butter, and eaten with apricot jam. The butter is not very Chinese, but the taste is stupendous.

ALMOND CUSTARD

This is a kind of compromise recipe: Chinese cooks would not use fresh milk, but I wouldn't use rennet. Compromise.

1 quart milk
1 cup almond meal (Available at gourmet stores, or grind your own in the blender.)
   sugar to taste, about 3 tablespoons
1 envelope unflavored gelatin

Heat the milk and the almond meal together just to simmering. Do not let the milk boil. Keep very warm but not boiling for 20 minutes. Strain the mixture through two thicknesses of cheesecloth. (Wring out what is left to extract all flavor possible from the almond meal.) Sweeten sparingly to taste.

Soften the gelatin in a little cold water, then add to the milk-almond mixture. Heat until the gelatin is completely dissolved but do not boil.

Pour the custard into individual serving dishes and put them in the refrigerator to chill and set. The mixture will not be very firm, just thickened. Serve very cold with orange flower syrup to pour over the junket, if you like.

ORANGE FLOWER SYRUP

Combine 2 tablespoons cold water, 2 tablespoons orange water, and 2 tablespoons sugar and stir until the sugar is dissolved. Add another ¼ cup orange water. More sugar may be added if a sweeter syrup is desired. If a heavy syrup is needed, boil equal parts of sugar and water together for 5 minutes; let cool and add 1 part orange water.

SESAME COOKIES

2 ¼ cups flour
   1 teaspoon baking powder
   ½ cup sugar
   ⅔ cup lard
   1 egg
   1 tablespoon water
   1 teaspoon vanilla extract
   ⅔ cup sesame seeds

Heat the oven to 400° F. Sift the dry ingredients together. Cut in the lard until the mixture looks like coarse meal. Beat the egg slightly with the water and vanilla extract and add all at once to the dry mixture. Stir and knead until a smooth dough is formed.

Roll out the dough very thin on a floured board and cut it in circles or fancy shapes. Place on a baking sheet, ungreased, and brush with the yolk of one egg beaten with 1 tablespoon of water to make a glaze. Sprinkle generously with sesame seeds and bake until light brown. The cookies will not be crisp when they come from the oven, so test them by the color. As they cool, and the shortening hardens, they will become crisp.

GLAZED WALNUTS

1 ½ cups sugar
 ½ cup corn syrup
 ½ cup water
 ¼ teaspoon salt
 1 tablespoon oil
 2 cups walnut meats

Cook the sugar, syrup, water, and salt to 300° F. on a candy thermometer (hard-crack stage). Remove from heat and stir in oil. Dip walnut pieces into the syrup in a slotted spoon or a sieve. Drain and turn out on waxed paper. Separate with chopsticks or a fork and let dry. Store in a tightly covered jar at room temperature (for a few days) or in the refrigerator (for longer storage).

Glazed Walnuts are not exactly a dessert; they are nice, however, after a meal, especially when served with brandy or a liqueur.

Other nuts may be glazed by the same method. Select pretty unbroken nut meats for glazing.

HELPFUL HINTS

Anise seed   This spice tastes like licorice without, of course, the sweet component of the candy. Anise seed is used widely in Chinese cooking, both in meat dishes and in desserts. Your author does not like it and has cravenly left it out of the recipes in this book. You may like it fine, however, so use it as desired. But sparingly because it is quite strong. A few seeds in vegetable dishes give an interesting flavor (in cabbage, for instance); slow-cooked meats may also take on added flavor and interest if a few anise seeds are added to the cooking liquid. Anise-flavored cookies or rice pudding are very good, too, providing you like the flavor to start with.

Bean curd   Since this book was begun, the author has found that canned bean curd is available both from Trinacria and Moneo's in New York City (see Sources for details). It is a delicious and nutritious addition to many dishes. For instance, add about 1 cup bean curd cut in 1″ x ½″ pieces to stir-fry dishes. Allow it just enough time to heat through, perhaps 2 or 3 minutes. A simple and delicious dish would be sliced pork, scallions and bean curd. You will think of many more combinations.

Freezing   If you have a freezer, you can make a big splash in Chinese cooking indeed. Stock can be made when the ingredients are on hand, then degreased, and frozen until needed. Slow-cooked meat dishes can be frozen in their broth, then defrosted and the dish finished whenever it is needed. In general if there are several components (meat, vegetables, etc.) in a dish, it is better to freeze them separately and combine them after defrosting to make the finished dish. Fresh greens cook so fast that they can be added as they would be in a recipe you were making from scratch.

Do remember that even frozen foods don't last forever; declare a feast and clean out the freezer every six months or so.

Garlic   Garlic is so important to Chinese cooking that it deserves some additional comment. First, buy it in as small quantities as you find practical. Garlic *can* get stale, and then it imparts a flavor that nobody can love! Make sure the cloves of garlic are tight and hard when you buy them. Store them in the refrigerator in a tightly-covered small glass jar. (Do not wash the garlic, of course.) Use it up fast. If you suspect the garlic on hand is over the hill, peel a clove and look at it. If it is dry and dark, it is sure to have an extremely odd smell. Discard it; a tiny piece can turn a big pot of something delicious into a disaster. It might be handy to keep on hand a jar of freeze-dried garlic bits to use in such emergencies; they won't give quite as good a taste as really fresh garlic, but will be better than garlic that has gone to its reward.

Monosodium glutamate   This chemical flavor-enhancer has been abused by many Chinese restaurants and by many home cooks as well. It is true that a judicious sprinkle may revive the taste of leftovers and vegetables past their prime; it is also true that too much of it is what makes That Famous Brand of soup taste alike in all varieties. In addition, some people seem to get unpleasant physical reactions from too much MSG (the Chinese-Restaurant Syndrome). In Szechuan dishes, there is usually plenty of tasty flavoring. In general I would say you would never need MSG in the recipes in this book. If you do decide to use some, go easy.

Pressure cookers   Most Chinese dishes cook so fast that a pressure cooker would be more of a hindrance than a help. For slow-cooked meats and broths, however, a cooker can reduce the overall cooking time significantly. Follow the recipes that come with your cooker, or allow about 5 minutes at 15 pounds pressure, then 30 minutes of standing for chunks of meat, longer cooking and standing for larger pieces such as whole pork shoulders. When the standing time is over (and the pressure is completely down!), open the pot and complete the dish. This method is sort of semi-fast since it speeds up the long, slow cooking of the meat but leaves the vegetables to cook as usual. I have had better luck this way, though; pressure cookers and vegetables are a tricky combination indeed.

Sprouts   The sprouts in dishes in restaurants are usually pea sprouts instead of soy bean sprouts. Between the time this book was started and now, kits have become available everywhere that provide seed, growing media, proper containers—everything to grow sprouts at home. Canned sprouts were always available, but they bore the same relationship to fresh ones that canned spaghetti does to *al dente*. If you like sprouts, by all means use them in place of or in addition to leafy vegetables in the recipes in this book. Not only are sprouts delicious and very Chinese, they are also extremely nutritious.

Steamers The ideal steamer for most dishes would be a big lovely stock pot deep enough to hold anything you can imagine wanting to cook, a rack to fit into it, and a good tight lid. Unfortunately, there is no getting around that such an arrangement is quite expensive and bulky to store during all those nonsteaming times. Any deep pot that will hold the dish to be steamed and a rack to keep it out of the water will do. You can improvise a foil lid if necessary.

A very handy steamer can be made from your wok if you get the rack that corresponds to its size. It will be a flat, perforated disk that will fit about one-third up from the bottom of the wok. The liquid goes in the bottom, the food to be steamed on the disk, and the big lid goes over all. It is amazing how much food to be steamed even a moderate-sized wok will hold this way. And if it is necessary to add more liquid, it can easily be poured down the side of the wok without the danger of sloshing it over the steaming food. So, when you buy a wok, be sure to get the rack. If you (like me) did not get a rack at first, ask for one nicely and perhaps the store can order it for you. Or if you know someone handy with tinsnips, you can have one made. Very useful.

Vitamin E For deep frying, the oil will stay fresh and nonrancid for several cookings if you add the contents of a 200-unit capsule of Vitamin E to the oil before you begin heating it the first time. The Vitamin E is completely tasteless and harmless and it will make a lot of difference in the amount of oil you need to buy for deep frying. It will also prevent the unpleasant taste that foods cooked in stale fat have. Of course, use your thermometer to make sure the fat is the proper temperature; too much heat destroys the oil and will cook the crust of food before the inside has a chance to get done.

Vitamin E is also the very best first-aid remedy for kitchen burns (after you have let very cold water run on them). Just pierce the capsule and squeeze the contents directly on the wound. I was skeptical about this, but I tried it and it really works.

Wok When you buy a new wok, it will need to be seasoned (as does a new black iron skillet) so food won't stick to it and so that so much fat will not be necessary in cooking. Your wok will probably have instructions with it; if so, use them. If not, try this method: wash, rinse, and dry the wok thoroughly. Brush it inside with *fresh* unsalted fat and heat until the fat is very hot but not smoking. Reduce the heat to the minimum and let the wok stay hot for at least 30 minutes. Wipe out any excess fat standing on the surface and let the wok cool. Repeat once or twice more. Do not wash the wok with soap while the seasoning is going on. Just wipe it thoroughly with clean paper towels. Be sure to use fresh fat and not to let that fat burn. Otherwise you will have imparted two unpleasant tastes to your wok more or less forever. If the worst should happen, let the wok cook, wipe it out, wash with hot soapy water, scour with steel wool (if it is *really* bad), rinse, dry, and start all over.

Some experts tell you never to wash a wok with soap and water, just as some very good cooks advise never washing an omelet pan. Well . . . the time comes. I've never had any trouble at all after washing a well-seasoned wok or omelet pan. Just don't scour with steel wool or gritty cleanser. For minor clean-ups (such as between two dishes that are quite similar anyway), a Chinese pot scrubber that looks like a whiskbroom is very handy; just splash some hot water into the wok, scrub it around the sides with the brush, and toss it out. You'll be ready to go again!

Some utensils especially made to use with woks are convenient though by no means essential. You may want to get a large flat perforated skimmer—the very thing for retrieving frying pieces or solids from soups. A stirring spoon with one straight side and one curved one is helpful, too. Cooking chopsticks are convenient if you find them comfortable to use, and a wire strainer with a long handle is good for deep frying.

SOURCES

Two of the best sources of ingredients for Szechuan cooking are not Chinese at all, but they have a good selection of hard-to-find groceries and are reliable and fast about filling mail orders.

Trinacria Importing Company, 415 Third Avenue, New York, New York 10016. This marvelous store carries a very full selection of ingredients for Chinese dishes, including fresh and dried (mailable) coriander, fresh ginger, canned bamboo shoots, bean curd, dried chestnuts, dried mushrooms, dried shrimp, and dried and canned hot peppers. Also in stock are the spices for making your own curries and other Indian dishes from scratch and a serious selection of pots and pans. Trinacria also sells large cans of some vegetables and fruits, and even by mail you should save quite a lot on enough artichoke hearts or brandied peaches, say, to serve a large group.

To order, write your requests and send with your name, address (be sure to include the zip code since parcel post charges are calculated from zip codes), and a check or money order for the estimated cost of the order (no C.O.D.s). Trinacria will send you what they have that is mailable and within the deposit you sent. At this time there is not a catalog, but letters of inquiry will be answered if you enclose a stamped self-addressed envelope. You will be amazed at the variety of Trinacria's stock; if you want it, they probably have it. If you are in New York, by all means go by and have one of their legendary hero sandwiches (to take out) and meet the wonderful people who run the store. Also look over the selection of cheeses; you are sure to leave loaded down!

Casa Moneo Spanish Imports, 210 West 14th Street, New York, New York 10011. This store specializes in foods and all kinds of merchandise from Mexico and other Latin countries. They will fill mail orders for chilis (dried and canned), spices, cookware, and anything else mailable they have in stock C.O.D. (minimum order $5.00, including postage) and send a catalog at the same time. Be sure to include your name, address, and zip code. If you are in New York, you will want to go by to look at the vast selection of sausages and cheeses, Spanish confections, canned goods, jewelry, and the latest Latin records.

INDEX